A NATION FIGHTS BACK

The Depression and Its Aftermath

The years from the stock market crash in 1929 to the New Deal, which began in 1933, were filled with fear, hunger, despair and social unrest as the nation was held in the grip of a great depression. Unemployment was at its peak with over 14,000,000 people out of work. Foreign trade collapsed. Agriculture was at its lowest ebb, with falling food prices. Banks failed daily and lifetime savings were wiped out. There was doubt and futility everywhere during the tragic, troublesome, desperate years of the early '30's. Then suddenly a strong voice echoed across America. "This nation will endure as it has endured, will revive and will prosper. . . . The only thing we have to fear is fear itself. . . ." That was the voice of Franklin Delano Roosevelt, as he faced the nation on Inauguration Day, March 4, 1933. To the homeless, the hopeless, the jobless, this spelled the dawn of a new era. With clarity and objectivity, the author traces the causes, the effects, the heartbreak and the slow climb back to normalcy as a nation fights to uphold the democratic way of life.

BOOKS BY IRVING WERSTEIN

Young Adult

MARSHAL WITHOUT A GUN: Tom Smith

MAN AGAINST THE ELEMENTS:
Adolphus W. Greely

CIVIL WAR SAILOR

1776: THE ADVENTURE OF THE AMERICAN
REVOLUTION TOLD WITH PICTURES

1861–1865: THE ADVENTURE OF THE CIVIL WAR
TOLD WITH PICTURES

THE BATTLE OF MIDWAY

THE MANY FACES OF THE CIVIL WAR

THE BATTLE OF AACHEN

A NATION FIGHTS BACK: The Depression and
Its Aftermath

Adult

JULY, 1863

ABRAHAM LINCOLN VERSUS JEFFERSON DAVIS

THE BLIZZARD OF '88

KEARNY THE MAGNIFICENT

A
NATION
FIGHTS BACK

The
Depression
and Its
Aftermath

by
Irving Werstein

Julian Messner, Inc.
New York

Published by Julian Messner, Inc.
8 West 40th Street, New York 18

Published simultaneously in Canada
by The Copp Clark Publishing Co. Limited

Photographs used with the permission
of Library of Congress, Wide World
Photos, United Press International
and The New-York Historical Society

Printed in the United States of America

Library of Congress Catalog Card No. 62-16676

This book is for Mamy Bogaert, a gallant lady of Brussels, Belgium, who always has known that there is nothing to fear but fear itself.

Contents

7

CONTENTS

PART THREE

DECADE OF DESPAIR AND HOPE, 1930–1940

8

Author's Note

I wish to thank the many people who have helped me in the completion of this book. The staff of The New-York Historical Society library was unceasingly kind and helpful; I thank Dr. James J. Heslin the Society's Director for his assistance and suggestions. Mr. Henry Chafetz and Mr. Sidney B. Solomon of the Pageant Book Company provided me with source material and personal reminiscences of the Depression. Mr. I. H. Wachtel, Washington, D.C., took time from his busy law practice to recall Depression experiences we had mutually shared. Mr. John G. Sturges supplied me with interesting data about the Stock Market Panic of 1929.

There were others who helped by refreshing my own memories of those harrowing days in the 1930's when my generation seemed hopelessly and irretrievably lost. I now thank all those friends for evoking remembrances.

To my editors, Miss Gertrude Blumenthal and Miss Lee Hoffman, I owe especial gratitude. It was they who unerringly uncovered the flaws in my work. Few authors can see for themselves the defects in a manuscript anymore than a parent can see the faults in his child. There is another reason to thank my editors: I am grateful for having been given the opportunity to write about a time in history in which I participated.

I believe that anyone who lived through the 1930's will never forget those trying days. They were a crucible, a furnace—and yet, despite the despair, they were days of uplift and striving, a period of essential honesty and moral courage.

Life was hard for most young people in the 1930's. It was a strange time to graduate from high school, to enter college, to hunt for a job, to come of age—but in the darkness there was still light. As Franklin D. Roosevelt put it, "Failure is not an American habit."

At the last I thank my agent, Miss Candida Donadio, for guidance, patience and sympathy. My wife, as always, gave me encouragement and my young son, Jack, did not try to coax me into games during working hours.

I. W.

New York, June 1962

10

A NATION FIGHTS BACK

The Depression and Its Aftermath

I

INAUGURATION DAY

Saturday, March 4, 1933

"We do not distrust the future of essential democracy. The people of the United States have not
failed. . . . They have asked for discipline and
leadership. . . . They have made me the present
instrument of their wishes. . . . In the spirit of the
gift I take it. . . ."

> FRANKLIN DELANO ROOSEVELT
> First Inaugural Address
> March 4, 1933

I

"It's a darned good sign..."

In Washington, D.C., on the morning of the Big Day, March 4, 1933, a brisk wind snapped the flags along Pennsylvania Avenue and tore at the bunting that festooned the buildings. The gray skies disappointed the many thousands who had come to Washington for the Big Day—the inauguration of Franklin Delano Roosevelt as thirty-second President of the United States.

Not since the Civil War had the national capital known such crowds as those which had begun to arrive in the city on Ash Wednesday, March 1, by train, bus, car and airplane. Every incoming public conveyance was filled to capacity and private cars converging on Washington created a monstrous traffic snarl. The influx continued day and night until long after dark on Friday, March 3.

Among the visitors were governors, senators, congressmen and other dignitaries; but there were also job seekers, chiselers, ward heelers, political bosses, cardsharps, pickpockets, con men, opportunists and even plain citizens.

A new administration was taking over. For the first time since Woodrow Wilson's re-election in 1916, the Democrats had another successful presidential candidate. The Republicans were out after an unbroken thirteen-year reign that had begun in 1920.

The Democrats swept the 1932 election by a 7,000,000 vote plurality, 22,000,000 to 15,000,000. The electoral vote, 472 to 59, made it a landslide over Herbert Hoover and Charles Curtis, the incumbent GOP President and Vice-President. Ironically, Franklin D. Roosevelt, the winner, had been the losing Democratic vice-presidential candidate in the 1920 election. This time, with John Nance Garner as his running mate, he whipped the Republicans.

Small wonder that so many Democrats had come to see the inaugural ceremonies. They had been waiting a long time for something to celebrate.

By March 3, all hotels in Washington were crammed. Cots had to be set up in lobbies and corridors. Lodging-house beds and furnished rooms for ten miles around Washington were renting at premium rates, and still there were not enough accommodations.

The police offered space in local jails to those who did not mind spending a night in a cell. School gymnasiums, church basements and armories were thrown open. The army provided canvas folding cots, and the Red Cross supplied coffee and doughnuts to the hungry, weary visitors. The Pennsylvania Railroad and the Baltimore & Ohio lined dozens of Pullman cars along rail sidings and permitted ticket holders to bed down in them. Despite all this, thousands slept on park benches, or napped in public libraries and

16

movie theatres. Others simple stayed awake, wandering the streets.

Business had never been better and money was spent unstintingly on food and souvenirs. Observers estimated that since March 1, between 200,000 and 300,000 people had been added to the city's population of a half million.

Few really minded the discomforts and inconveniences caused by the overcrowding: certainly not the gamblers who kept marathon poker games going in smoke-filled hotel rooms. The overworked metropolitan police could not cope with the hordes of pickpockets, and hundreds of unwary inauguration spectators were plucked clean.

Although Inauguration Days were usually inclement, everyone hoped Roosevelt would have good weather. There had not been a sunny inaugural since March 4, 1921, when Harding was sworn in. But spirits lowered only slightly on March 4, 1933, as the day dawned with a threat of rain.

"You can't have everything," a leading Democrat philosophized. "Winning the election is enough. We have plenty of sunshine in our hearts."

Preparations for the ceremonies started shortly after daybreak as security forces moved into position. The metropolitan police were reinforced by scores of secret service agents, a specially picked detachment of one hundred New York City uniformed policemen and an equal number of detectives. Four hundred United States Marines, rifles loaded, bayonets fixed, deployed along Pennsylvania Avenue and stood guard from the White House to the Capitol.

The authorities were running no risks with FDR. They already had frightening evidence of how easily his life could be endangered.

At 9:00 P.M., Wednesday, February 15, only two weeks

earlier, Roosevelt had landed at Miami Beach, Florida, after a short fishing vacation on his friend Vincent Astor's yacht, the *Nourmahal*. The vessel berthed at the Bay Front Park pier where a large crowd waited to greet the President-elect. Also at hand to welcome their leader were a number of high-ranking Democrats, among them Anton Cermak, the mayor of Chicago.

Sun-tanned and fit, Roosevelt made a brief speech to the people. Amid a burst of applause, Cermak and others escorted FDR to an open touring automobile which was to lead a motor cavalcade through Miami Beach. Just as FDR reached the car, five shots cracked out in rapid succession.

At the first report, Mayor Cermak threw himself in front of Roosevelt to shield him. A bullet intended for FDR struck Cermak in the chest. He collapsed in Roosevelt's arms and murmured, "I'm glad it wasn't you!" Before the flurry of shooting ended, four persons lay wounded. But due to Cermak's courageous act, Roosevelt remained unharmed.

Police, secret servicemen and civilians pounced on the would-be assassin, a pint-sized man named Giuseppe Zangara. He had been only fifteen feet from FDR when he opened fire. Fortunately, his aim had been deflected by a Miami housewife standing next to him. She had grabbed his wrist and Zangara hit Cermak instead. It took swift police work to prevent the enraged crowd from lynching the half-demented man who kept screaming, "I hate all rulers! I hate all rich and powerful men! Kings! Bankers! Presidents!" His senseless act was the reason for all the extra precautions being taken on that inaugural morning.

Policemen and plainclothesmen patrolled rooftops along the route. Only at Lincoln's first inauguration in March 1861 had greater military safeguards been provided. Troops ringed the platform on the Capitol portico where the swearing-in ceremonies were to be held. Cavalry units were posted nearby to quell any disturbance, while tanks and armored cars stood ready. The security measures were complete by 9:00 A.M. Now there was nothing left to do but wait until 12:45 P.M. when Roosevelt would be sworn in by Chief Justice Charles Evans Hughes.

Long before that hour people streamed into Capitol Square. The throng before the Capitol was so dense that a police official remarked, "You'd need a shoehorn to squeeze a midget into that mob."

By noon, 150,000 persons jammed the square. Another 500,000 spectators, six deep, lined Pennsylvania Avenue.

Across the nation, millions of Americans grouped around radios to hear the proceedings; and untold numbers around the world could listen to the ceremony, broadcast by short wave.

About 10:30 A.M., a shattering roar arose from the on-lookers. The clouds suddenly parted and the sun shone brightly. The once somber day now sparkled with spring-like radiance.

"It's a darned good sign. FDR's going to be a lucky President," a man in the crowd stated sagely.

"After these last few years, we all could use some luck," another spectator remarked sourly.

19

2

"...unreasoning, unjustified terror..."

At 11:05 an open black limousine carrying the President-elect, Mrs. Roosevelt and several presidential aides, swung into the White House driveway. By tradition FDR should have entered the mansion to pay a formal call on Herbert Hoover, his outgoing predecessor.

However, Roosevelt was crippled and walked with great difficulty. In August 1921, at the age of thirty-nine, he came down with polio. Now he wore heavy steel braces and walked with canes or crutches.

Hoover graciously came out to the car and spared FDR the ordeal of moving. After chatting a few moments with his successor, President Hoover took a seat in the vehicle and the motorcade moved on toward the Capitol.

Secret service agents trotted alongside the limousine. A

cordon of mounted police surrounded it. The motor cavalcade proceeded up Pennsylvania Avenue amid prolonged
cheers and applause. Roosevelt, flashing a smile that was
to become famous, doffed his silk top hat in response, but
Hoover remained stolid and solemn, paying no attention
to the applause.

The departing President must have known the ovation
was not meant for him. He was aware that he was being
blamed for the unhappy conditions in America. During his
administration, which lasted from March 1929 to March
1933, the worst economic depression in American history
gripped the nation.

As a result of the bad situation in the United States there
was a world-wide business collapse that brought on unrest,
poverty, unemployment and discontent in almost every country, particularly in Europe where American influences were
strongest.

Across the Atlantic, France and England struggled to stave
off bankruptcy. Thousands of once proud Britons now lived
on public welfare, a pitifully inadequate dole handed out
by a grudging government. Unemployment was high and
privation great, especially in the industrial Midlands and the
coal mining regions of Wales.

France was torn by rioting as hungry workers demanded
jobs and bread. In Germany, millions hailed Adolf Hitler
who had just been appointed Chancellor by the Reich's senile
President, Paul von Hindenburg. Hitler's National Socialist
(Nazi) Party had become Germany's dominant political
force as a result of the Reichstag elections in February 1933.

Hitler, the self-styled German *Fuehrer* (Leader) proclaimed that he had been divinely chosen not only to free
his people from the "chains" of the Versailles Treaty which

had ended World War I but also to save the Fatherland from Bolshevism.

At the very moment the shiny limousines were roaring up Pennsylvania Avenue for the time-honored American ritual of swearing in a new President, wide areas of the world were embroiled in war and violence. Far away in the Jehol Province of Northern China, a Japanese army had captured the provincial capital, Changteh, after routing the poorly led defenders. This latest step in the Nipponese plans for the conquest of all Asia was part of an aggression begun in 1931 when Japan had seized Manchuria.

By March 1933, another war had broken out, this one in South America where Paraguay and Bolivia were fighting over a strip of territory in the tin-rich Chaco region that bordered both countries. In the Caribbean, Cuba was aflame with revolutionary activity against her military dictator, Gerardo Machado. There was turmoil, violence and despair everywhere in 1933.

Even the rich and powerful United States had not escaped, for on the day Roosevelt was inaugurated over 14,000,000 able-bodied Americans were unemployed, with no hope of finding jobs. Thousands of the jobless had no money and no means of support.

In this climate of confusion, bewilderment and unhappiness, Franklin D. Roosevelt prepared to take office. He radiated confidence as he raised his top hat to the cheering throngs. He was about to face problems more crucial than any that had confronted all his predecessors, with the possible exception of Abraham Lincoln, who came to the Presidency as the country hovered on the brink of civil war.

It was Roosevelt's task to inspire the dispirited people and rekindle their will to fight. "Failure is not an American

22

habit," he had insisted throughout the 1932 election campaign. He was himself living proof that a man could struggle against odds and win.

He had been written off by political experts in August 1921. "Franklin Roosevelt is through," was the general opinion.

After all, a polio-crippled man could not engage in politics, some believed. It was too bad, they moaned, the Democratic party needed candidates of FDR's caliber. He had shown a flair for public life and possessed great executive abilities.

As Assistant Secretary of the Navy, during World War I, Roosevelt had revealed a talent for leadership. It was his performance in that post which brought him the vice-presidential nomination during the 1920 election. Although Roosevelt was not a winner then, his bold campaigning earned him national recognition.

Franklin Delano Roosevelt was born January 30, 1882, at his parents' home in Hyde Park, New York. The only son of James and Sara Delano Roosevelt, young Franklin enjoyed a comfortable childhood. He had the material advantages that went with being a rich man's son. His father was a successful businessman and very wealthy, although the elder Roosevelt did not believe money-making to be the prime purpose of his life.

In fact, James Roosevelt's main interest was Springwood, his Hyde Park estate. Because he loved the place so deeply, he retired from business at a fairly early age and devoted himself to looking after his house and land. As a result, the Roosevelts were not millionaires; yet there was money enough for Franklin to have private tutors, for servants and a household staff, and for long, pleasant vacations abroad each year.

It was in this atmosphere of ease and luxury that young Franklin grew to adolescence. His mother, Sara, doted on her son. She often asserted her belief that Franklin was destined for greatness and saved everything connected with him —letters, notes, photographs—as though keeping them secure for posterity.

When he was fourteen, Franklin entered Groton and in 1900 matriculated at Harvard, from which he graduated in June 1904. During his junior year at college, he fell in love with a distant cousin, Anna Eleanor Hall Roosevelt, and decided she was the girl he wanted to be his wife.

After enrolling at Columbia Law School, he proposed to Eleanor and they were married March 17, 1905, in New York. FDR practiced law for a while and in 1910 took his first plunge into politics. He was elected state senator from Hyde Park, the first Democrat to win that seat in more than thirty years.

Roosevelt enjoyed politics. During the 1912 presidential election he worked hard for Woodrow Wilson. As a reward for his efforts, President Wilson appointed him Assistant Secretary of the Navy, a post tailor-made for the handsome young man from Hyde Park. Roosevelt had loved ships all his life and was an expert naval historian as well as a fine small-boat sailor.

When the United States entered the World War in 1917, FDR won high praise for his effective work with the Navy. By the time the war was over, Roosevelt had become an important national figure, and when the Democrats selected James M. Cox of Ohio as their 1920 candidate, thirty-eight-year-old Franklin Delano Roosevelt was the delegates' nearly unanimous choice for Cox's running mate.

Roosevelt proved to be a sound choice. An aristocrat, he

had the common touch; eloquent, he could be appreciated by college professors as well as truck drivers. He came from the right background—blue-blood family with connections in high places, yet not too snobbish. Roosevelt was rich enough to be beyond temptation but he was no multimillionaire. Accepted among capitalists, he was also regarded as a friend by labor.

Still, back in 1921 the Democratic political bosses believed FDR was finished despite all his qualifications for high office. Polio had wrecked his career. This perhaps might have been true of a lesser man, not so FDR. He actually vanquished the cruel disease, crawling first then walking.

Just seven years after his illness Franklin Roosevelt was elected governor of New York State, a post he won again in 1930. Two years later, in November 1932, he gained the Presidency of the United States. His was the sort of courage Americans admired. As one ordinary citizen noted, "FDR came up to bat with two strikes against him and belted the next pitch right out of the park."

If the President could beat polio, then Americans could lick the Depression. Like Roosevelt, the country was at bat with two strikes against it. But there was still a chance to blast a homer.

In Roosevelt, Americans believed they had a man who meant to do more than speak longingly of a vanished prosperity that was always tantalizingly "just around the corner." FDR had promised to give the country a New Deal. No matter what that might turn out to be, it could be no worse than the "Raw Deal" the people had been getting since 1930.

So it was that at 1:08 in the afternoon of March 4, 1933, Franklin Delano Roosevelt placed his left hand on a Bible,

raised his right hand and faced Chief Justice Charles Evans
Hughes in the climactic moment of the ceremony.

The notables crowded on the platform and the huge
throng in Capitol Square listened attentively as Roosevelt's
voice rang clearly from the public address loudspeakers, re-
peating the oath administered by Justice Hughes, an oath
that officially made him President: "I do solemnly swear
that I will faithfully execute the office of the President of the
United States . . . so help me God!"

The strong, determined voice echoed across the square.
Picked up by radio transmitters it was broadcast to every part
of the United States and by short wave around the world.

A few moments later, before the same battery of microphones, FDR delivered his inaugural address. Although he
had shed topcoat and hat, the President was unmindful of
the sharp wind that rustled his papers and ruffled his hair
as he gripped the lectern to steady himself. The sunlight
glinted off his pince-nez glasses. His patrician face was sternly
set and his voice did not falter as he said:

> . . . this is pre-eminently the time to speak the truth, the
> whole truth, frankly and boldly. . . . Nor need we shrink
> from honestly facing conditions in our country today. This
> great nation will endure as it has endured, will revive and
> will prosper. So first of all let me assert my firm belief that
> the only thing we have to fear is fear itself—nameless, unrea-
> soning, unjustified terror which paralyzes needed efforts to
> convert retreat into advance. . . ."

⌐ 3

"Where do we go from here, boys?"

After finishing his speech, the President left the Capitol accompanied by his family, cabinet members and aides. The presidential party proceeded to a special grandstand on Pennsylvania Avenue from which FDR was to review the parade. Eleanor Roosevelt, the First Lady, resplendent in a dress of "Eleanor blue," a shade named for her, sat beside her husband in a section of the stand enclosed by bulletproof glass.

The inaugural parade was long and impressive. Some 18,000 marchers, including Democratic party dignitaries, floats, bands, sailors, soldiers, marines, cavalry and a young boy from Chula, Georgia, who had ridden more than 800 miles on a pony to be there, took part in the parade.

Overhead planes of the Army Air Corps performed daredevil maneuvers. The President seemed to be enjoying himself enormously, watching with interest the planes and the units in the line of march. The parade went off without a hitch, although about four hundred persons in the crowd required medical assistance for one reason or another.

The most serious mishap of the day occurred in a low flying "blimp" carrying newspaper cameramen. One photographer snapping pictures from the rear of the airship's gondola leaned over so far that his hand and camera were mashed by a propeller blade.

Besides the parade, several other celebratory events had been planned, but most of them were canceled out of deference to FDR's longtime friend, Senator Thomas J. Walsh, who had been stricken on March 3 by a fatal heart attack aboard a train en route to the capital. Walsh was to have served in the cabinet as Attorney General.

FDR managed to conceal his deepfelt sorrow, but those close to him knew how much he had been affected by Walsh's death.

Still, the business of government could not wait on sentiment. A new Attorney General, Homer S. Cummings, was appointed to take his place on the reviewing stand with the other cabinet members: Cordell Hull, Secretary of State; Daniel Roper, Secretary of Commerce; William H. Woodin, Secretary of the Treasury; Frances Perkins, Secretary of Labor (the first woman ever appointed to a cabinet post); George H. Dern, Secretary of War; Senator Claude Swanson, Secretary of the Navy; Harold Ickes, Secretary of the Interior and James Farley, Postmaster General.

After the inaugural parade, FDR returned to the White House to attend the traditional inaugural ball. Just as the Roosevelts were about to leave for the affair, the sad news came that Mayor Cermak had slipped into a coma and was close to death. Again FDR had to hide his feelings, which he did so successfully that none of the celebrants at the ball guessed the President's sorrow as he made a smiling entrance and waved to them from the presidential box.

The ball was a success. Everyone had a good time but there was a note of irony during the festivities. At one point the dance band struck up a tune called "Where Do We Go from Here, Boys?" that had been popular back in 1917. It was an appropriate air, for that question occurred to many Americans on the night the Roosevelt era began. Sure, FDR had made a terrific speech—but where do we go from here, boys? Where do we go from here?

II

THE HIGH, WIDE
AND HANDSOME YEARS

1919–1929

{ "We shall soon be . . . within sight of the day when\
 poverty will be abolished from the nation. . . ."

> PRESIDENT HERBERT HOOVER /
> June 1929

II

THE HIGH, WIDE
AND HANDSOME YEARS

1919-1929

1

"How ya gonna keep 'em down on the farm...?"

The trail that led FDR to the White House in 1933, twisted back to the end of the Great War of 1914–1918 and the clamorous days of the so-called Roaring Twenties. The seeds of the Depression were sown in the helter-skelter decade that followed the war—a conflict the United States had entered with the idealistic vision of "making the world safe for democracy."

Americans marched off to war singing "Over There" and "Goodbye Broadway, Hello France" in the belief that this was to be the "War to end War." The whole country pitched in to win the struggle. There were Meatless Tuesdays, Lightless Wednesdays, Sugarless Thursdays.

Schoolchildren saved tin foil and collected junk which could be converted into guns and ammunition. Everyone bought Liberty Bonds and movie stars entertained the crowds in Times Square at mammoth Liberty Bond rallies.

For the first time since the terrible years of the Civil War, the nation was fighting in a major conflict. But the American people withstood the stress and the sacrifice. Except for the usual crop of war profiteers, Americans demonstrated to the world what a free, democratic country could do in a time of danger.

Then, at last, on November 11, 1918, it was over. Whistles blew, bells rang, people danced in the streets, pretty girls (and not such pretty ones) were kissed by boys in uniform. The delirious crowds hung a thousand effigies of the German Kaiser. They snake-danced up Broadway, in Chicago's Loop, on every Main Street, shouting "The war's over! It's really over!"

That tumultuous Monday in November 1918, no one in the joyous throngs dreamed that after only twenty-three years and twenty-six days of peace the United States would again be at war. No one on that Armistice Day would have believed that the conflict just ended was one day to be known as the First World War because there would be a second, more terrible one.

Had not this been the war to end war? Surely after all the slaughter and the devastation, nations were through with killing forever—now all men could be brothers.

But the brotherhood of man was only a future dream. Present reality presented problems and one was the obvious fact that the war had altered the accepted American "way of life."

A team of songwriters in New York's Tin Pan Alley had enough insight to recognize this. In 1919, they dashed off a catchy song that asked: "How Ya Gonna Keep 'em Down on the Farm, After They've Seen Paree?"

In snappy, slangy lyrics the song stressed the fact that

34

nothing would ever again be quite the same in the U.S.A., particularly for the 2,000,000 doughboys who had gone "Over There." In 1917, the Yanks had been wide-eyed, naïve innocents. Now, they were returning home after two years and no one could seriously expect young men who had strolled along the Champs Élysées and fought through the hell of the Argonne Forest to accept life on a small farm or in a "one horse" town as though nothing at all had happened.

The returning doughboy had seen much, learned a lot and now demanded still more. He wanted thrills, excitement, experiences and money—heaps of it. And he went to the big cities to find them—Chicago, Detroit, San Francisco, New York—where opportunities were greater than back home. The old ways might still suit Grandpa, but Grandson was off to explore new frontiers. So the former doughboy shed his uniform and looked over the country he had left a year or so earlier.

Possibly the first thing he noticed was the increased cost of everything. Since 1917, rents had risen by 20 to 50 per cent. Clothing was more expensive and the dollar neither stretched so far as nor bought all it once had. Milk rose from nine to fifteen cents a quart. Sirloin steak sold for forty-two cents a pound—it had been twenty-seven. Butter, formerly priced at thirty-one cents a pound, prewar, had soared to sixty-one cents. Eggs, which now cost sixty-two cents a dozen, had gone for thirty-four cents in 1917.

But the returned soldier did not fret too much about prices. In the postwar world any man with "moxie"—which meant drive and ambition in the slang of the period—could see a bright future ahead.

New businesses were opening—take automobiles, for example. Back in '17, there had been only 3,000,000 cars as compared to 20,000,000 horses. Two years later, 9,000,000 autos were rattling, clattering and bumping over the country's rutted dirt roads. Sure, plenty of horses were still around, but a smart, fast-talking fellow could do worse than sell cars for a living or, if he happened to be mechanically inclined, go to work in an auto factory. Out in Detroit, Henry Ford was paying good wages and needed men to make his already famous Model T or "Tin Lizzie."

Not only Ford but many new automobile manufacturers as well were going into full production. Thousands of jobs were available in the booming industry. Experts predicted that by 1930 there would be 27,000,000 cars in use and a million miles of paved highways for them to travel on. All that seemed far-fetched in 1919, but who was to say what could happen in fast-moving America, where the sky was the limit?

All sorts of new products and industrial wonders were appearing on the horizon. People talked of marvels such as radios for home use. Imagine listening to music, a ball game or a play right in your own parlor! Also predicted for the near future were passenger-carrying airplanes with frequent service between cities. Telephones and electric lights in every home were soon to be realized.

One heard prophecies of electrically operated kitchen refrigerators to replace the old ice box. Also on the way were vacuum cleaners, electric washing machines, clothes driers, ranges, ovens, irons, toasters, percolators, and heating and cooling devices that would take the drudgery out of housework. The U.S.A. faced an era of limitless opportunities. It was a time to be young, dynamic and alert—a time for Americans to get ahead and make money.

36

Preoccupation with materialism caused most Americans to forget the idealism with which they had marched off to war in 1917. Now that the shooting was ended, they were more concerned about getting rich than with achieving President Woodrow Wilson's vision of a tranquil world made secure by a just peace and the elimination of war through a League of Nations.

For many years, even prior to the war, Wilson had advocated a "general association of nations" which would act as an arbiter in disputes between countries. He believed that mediation and not force of arms should settle international differences.

President Wilson's eloquent advocacy of a "just peace" had helped convince the German people they ought to surrender. Wilson insisted that the United States was fighting not against the people of Germany but only their imperialistic government. It was his belief that the war should not be followed by punitive measures against Germany. According to him, the peace ought to be based on the Fourteen Points of his program.

Wilson's Fourteen Points included such proposals as open treaties, openly arrived at; freedom of the seas, both in peace and war; no reparations; the reduction of armaments and the self-determination of all peoples. Wilson also insisted that "henceforth peace be maintained by the establishment of the rule of law in international affairs and a League of Nations to enforce it."

Unfortunately neither Great Britain nor France had ever formally accepted Wilson's Fourteen Points as their war aims. However, most people believed the American President was speaking for all the Allies.

In order to gain his objectives, President Wilson went to

France in December 1918, as the United States representative to the peace conference at Versailles, near Paris. The masses of Europe hailed Wilson as a hero, the white-armored champion of order and justice. They honored his Fourteen Points with a reverence usually reserved for the Ten Commandments. All the peoples of the war-ravaged continent looked upon Wilson as the savior of mankind.

But the spokesmen for the victorious Allies, England's Lloyd George, Georges Clemenceau, "The Tiger of France," and Victor Emanuel Orlando of Italy, unlike Wilson, were not visionaries but tough realists. They demanded a "hard peace"—Germany and the Germans must be made to pay for the war. These men sought vengeance, not justice, and if it appeared that their own people seemed to prefer Wilson's way, it made no difference to George, Clemenceau and Orlando. Practical politicians, they knew that sooner or later the cheers for Wilson would fade away. Idealism stood little chance against nationalism. The so-called Big Three continued to play on the hatred most of Europe felt toward Germany.

Mistrust, fear and suspicion held seats at the Versailles Conference as did the ghosts of the millions who had died to stop German aggression. All over Europe millions scrabbled for scraps of food in the war-ravaged towns and villages the Germans had destroyed. It was not easy to speak of justice to them.

Although Wilson still remained a popular figure in Europe, his voice alone could not check the fires hatred had kindled. As a result, the Versailles Treaty reflected almost nothing of Wilson's program or his Fourteen Points. Secret deals were made among nations. Germany was stripped of her colonies and forced to pay the full cost of the war—some

38

$33,000,000,000. The right of minorities to self-determination was denied in many parts of the continent when borders were shifted and new countries such as Czechoslovakia and Yugoslavia were created at the expense of Austria, Hungary, Turkey and Germany, the defeated powers.

Wilson did win one victory. At his insistence, the Versailles Treaty provided for the establishment of a League of Nations. The treaty was so worded that no nation could accept its terms without also agreeing to the establishment of the League. This clause had been inserted by Wilson because he knew that a strong isolationist sentiment was rising in the United States Senate, which had to ratify the treaty. By linking the treaty and League, Wilson had made certain that the isolationist senators could not reject one without rejecting the other.

The anti-treaty, anti-League forces in America were led by Senator Henry Cabot Lodge of Massachusetts, chairman of the Foreign Relations Committee, who seemed to be motivated more by his violent dislike of Wilson than by any objections to either the Versailles Treaty or the League of Nations. What Wilson favored, Lodge opposed. Wilson's political foes used the issue of American participation in the League as a means to discredit the President. They resorted to cheap, vicious smear tactics by spreading anti-League rumors that played on American fears: the League, they whispered, was a superstate that would rob the United States of its independence; enemies of the United States in the League would insist on American disarmament, thus leaving the nation at the mercy of any unscrupulous power; the colored races of the world would dominate the white races through the League; the whole world would be dominated by the

Roman Catholic Church, which was the main force behind the League of Nations, according to the rumor mongers.

This crude propaganda was given credence in the United States because the American people had developed an antipathy toward the war, the problems of Europe and the world. The war had cost them dearly in lives and money. One hundred and twenty-six thousand Americans had died from all causes, including battle casualties, while 234,000 had been wounded or injured between April 1917 and November 1918. In 1919, no one yet knew how many billions of dollars the war had cost America. As a result, the feeling was growing in the United States that the country had no business "getting involved in Europe again."

On the other hand, Wilson kept trying to bring the United States into the League of Nations, arguing that the League and peace treaty were indivisible—one could not survive without the other.

But his opponents in the Senate sneered at that concept. The League, they scoffed, was a bonehead idea dreamed up by do-gooders. It would never work. You could no more get the European powers to sit down together than you could dogs and cats. The League was hogwash. No true American wanted his country mixed up again with those rascal foreigners. All that bunch wanted was Uncle Sam's dollars. We had pulled the British and French chestnuts out of the fire in '17 and should've learned our lesson, which was "Stay out of Europe!"

Still, Wilson refused to give up. He came home and toured the country, speaking to crowds at railroad depots, in auditoriums and even on street corners, always pounding home the need for the League of Nations. Lodge and his

40

followers meanwhile bombarded the people with a steady barrage of the slogan, "No Foreign Entanglements!"

The battle raged until, taxed beyond endurance, Wilson fell ill on September 25, 1919, in Pueblo, Colorado. A special train sped him back to Washington. A few days later, the President suffered a stroke that paralyzed his left side and impaired his vocal chords.

He had lost his crusade.

For seventeen months Wilson remained an almost helpless invalid. The United States neither joined the League of Nations nor endorsed the Versailles Treaty but made a separate peace with Germany in 1921. Without America's strength and prestige the League proved impotent and no international organization of real strength existed to block future aggressions. Senator Lodge and the anti-Wilson bloc had won their shortsighted triumph—but it proved to be a bitter one, for out of it arose the Second World War.

Thus, the high-flown principles of Woodrow Wilson, the cherished hopes of a world from which war was forever banished, were blown away on the winds of deceit, narrowmindedness, greed and the lust for power.

Because some men had placed personal and political differences before national good, twice within a single generation much of the world was turned into a wasteland. And twice within that same generation Americans died on far-off battlefields.

⌐ 2

"The Bolsheviks
are taking over!"

As debate raged in the United States over the League of Nations and the Versailles Treaty, a wave of sudden fear gripped millions of otherwise levelheaded Americans. The fear had its roots in the Russian Revolution of 1917 in which the Communists, known in Russia as Bolsheviks, led by Nicolai Lenin and Leon Trotsky overthrew the Tsar and set up a Soviet government.

In 1919, similar uprisings occurred in several countries of Europe, and Americans began worrying that a "Red Plague" would somehow span the Atlantic Ocean to infest the United States.

A "Red Scare," launched by sensational newspapers, jingoists, superpatriots and self-seekers, threw the nation into a state of hysteria. Every liberal was labeled a "Bolshevik agent." Trade unionists were tagged "Reds." Unfounded spy plots, rumors of revolution, threats of sabotage sprang up on every hand. It was even said that Leon Trotsky, one of the leaders of the Russian Revolution, had been smuggled into the United States to mastermind a "Red Revolution" in America.

When a wave of strikes engulfed the country, American businessmen, great and small, were convinced that organized labor had entered a Red conspiracy to seize power. By mid-November 1919, just a year after the Armistice, more than 1,000,000 workers were on strike for higher wages to meet soaring living costs. Building trades workers, shoemakers, telephone operators, coal miners, steelworkers and even actors marched on picket lines.

But of all the strikes none caused more dismay than one that took place in Boston, Massachusetts. On September 9, 1919, that city's police force struck for higher wages. The men earned only $1,100 a year, out of which they had to buy uniforms. City officials had stubbornly refused to heed the policemen's demands and the police commissioner suspended nineteen men because they had circulated a petition which called for a pay boost.

The whole police force walked out in protest and not a single law enforcement officer remained on duty in all Boston. The mayor's call for volunteers to patrol the streets met with some response from Harvard undergraduates, ex-soldiers and white-collared Back Bay brokers. But this make-shift body could not deal with the upsurge of hoodlumism that terrorized the "city without cops." Criminals, toughs, rowdies and thieves roved about at will, breaking windows, looting stores and robbing pedestrians.

The mayor begged Calvin Coolidge, Governor of Massachusetts, to send the National Guard. State troops were

43

swiftly mobilized and rushed into Boston. Although soldiers patrolled the streets, it took several days before order could be restored. The newspapers handled the strike with a lack of good sense and restraint. Front-page stories and editorials wildly claimed that the Boston police walkout was the signal for a full-scale Red uprising.

"THE BOLSHEVIKS ARE TAKING OVER!" a Boston newspaper headline shrieked.

However, with the National Guard in town, the rowdies slunk back to their pool halls and beer parlors. The streets of Boston became safe again, and the striking policemen returned to work without having gained a single demand. The real winner of the unpleasant affair was sour-faced Calvin Coolidge who had declared: "There is no right to strike against the public safety by anybody, anywhere, anytime!"

His firm stand during the trouble brought Coolidge into national prominence. Republican party chiefs decided that the usually taciturn governor might make a good second man on the party's ticket in the 1920 presidential election.

The "Red Scare" stirred up tempests in Boston and Seattle, in New York and Chicago. Many believed Red agitation was responsible for the police strike, although its real cause was low wages. Every day hysteria rose higher. It reached a peak when packages containing bombs were mailed to several prominent persons. Two actually exploded—one maimed the servant of an anti-labor senator, the other partially wrecked the home of United States Attorney General A. Mitchell Palmer. Understandably, the bombing outrages aroused public indignation and the government lashed out at the radical movement.

Operating under a wartime Sedition Act, Attorney General Palmer initiated a series of anti-Red measures. On New

Year's Day, 1920, his agents raided radical headquarters, hangouts, bookshops and dwelling places. They rounded up scores of persons, many of whom were completely innocent. Palmer's overzealous agents even arrested pedestrians who merely happened to be passing a raided premises.

During January 1920, large-scale deportations of known left-wing aliens were carried out. One ship, with more than two hundred Communists aboard, was called the "Red Ark."

An unprecedented reactionary wave gripped the United States. Race riots flared between Negroes and whites in Chicago and elsewhere. Police, strikers and non-strikers fought pitched battles in a dozen cities. Duly elected officials were denied office only because they had run on the Socialist party ticket. The New York State Assembly expelled five such Socialists on the grounds that they were "agents of Red Russia," although the men had won their assembly seats in a strictly legal fashion at the polls.

It was not long before prominent Americans began to speak out against these excesses. Charles Evans Hughes, the 1916 Republican presidential candidate, was a distinguished jurist destined to be a future Secretary of State and, later, Chief Justice of the Supreme Court. He forcefully protested the expulsion of the New York Socialists as "unwarranted, unconstitutional and un-American." No one dared accuse Hughes of Red sympathies. Other men of Hughes' stature similarly condemned the hysteria.

The *New York World* editorialized: ". . . there is no Bolshevist menace in the United States . . . no anarchist menace, no socialist menace and no Red menace that an ordinarily competent police force cannot handle and deal with. . . ."

45

Attorney General Palmer, sensing a definitely growing disinterest in his holy war on the Reds, announced that he had learned from an unrevealed, but reliable source that a vast Bolshevik plot was in the making. On May Day, 1920, Palmer said, the Reds planned to unleash a wave of sabotage, arson and assassinations as a prelude to the revolution.

May Day passed placidly and tranquilly. Children danced around the May Pole on the Mall in Central Park. The sun shone brightly and only a few seedy soapbox orators harangued thin crowds.

"Palmer's Revolution" became a standing joke. Vaudeville comedians could break up an audience by screaming, "Comes the Revolution!" The crusading Attorney General had made a laughingstock of himself. The self-styled "Fighting Quaker" was derided as the "Quaking Fighter" and the "Quaker Faker." The Great Red Scare of 1920 evaporated in the laughter of a public that suddenly had regained both its equilibrium and sense of humor.

The people turned from Palmer's Red fantasies to more pressing issues. On January 17, 1920, the Eighteenth Amendment (Volstead Act) which made illegal "the sale and/or manufacture of alcoholic beverages in the United States" had gone into effect to usher in the gangsterism, racketeering and criminality of the Prohibition Era.

A few months later, the United States fully entered the twentieth century by granting women the right to vote with the Nineteenth Amendment, which became law on August 10, 1920. By midsummer, Americans were more interested in recipes for homemade gin or the telephone number of a dependable bootlegger than the Red Menace. To many, Prohibition was a menace far worse than Bolshevism.

People also wondered how the women's vote would affect

46

the presidential election in November. The candidates had already been chosen by both major parties. That year the Republicans picked a handsome, affable United States senator from Marion, Ohio, Warren G. Harding, to carry the GOP banner. Dour Calvin Coolidge was his running mate.

The Democrats gave the nod to the governor of Ohio, James M. Cox, a sincere but undistinguished man completely overshadowed by his vice-presidential candidate, Franklin D. Roosevelt.

So far had Palmer's "Red Scare" faded from the American scene that when a bomb was exploded on Wall Street in September 1920, even the lurid journals could not convince the public that the act was anything more than the work of a crackpot and not a vast Red masterplot.

The era of unreasoning hysteria had passed. The American people had regained enough faith in themselves to see that no revolutionary conspiracy could ever win the support of more than a handful of malcontents and fanatics. Only once again in the twenties was the nation to be aroused by controversy over radicalism.

In April 1920, at the height of the "Red Scare," two Italian anarchists, a fish peddler, Bartolomeo Vanzetti, and a shoemaker, Nicola Sacco, were sentenced to death on flimsy evidence for the killing of a paymaster during the holdup of a shoe factory in Braintree, Massachusetts.

At first, the trial attracted almost no attention. But left-wingers made the Sacco-Vanzetti case a *cause célèbre*. Anti-American riots on behalf of the condemned men erupted outside United States embassies throughout Europe and South America.

Since the two men had been sentenced without solid proof, American liberals took up their cause. The fight to save

47

Sacco and Vanzetti lasted seven years, until August 22, 1927, when they were electrocuted amid tumultuous scenes as their supporters rioted in almost every major American city and in a score of countries. Those who cared about Sacco and Vanzetti wept. The average American might have felt a bit uneasy about the results of the trial—seven years was a long time for the state to have taken to exact justice. But this was the day of quick money in the stock market, Babe Ruth was hitting homers almost at will, everything was fine in the U.S.A. And, after all, why should anyone worry about the fate of two anarchists—foreigners to boot?

☞ 3

"...not nostrums but normalcy..."

On Tuesday, November 2, 1920, more than 25,000,000 Americans went to the polls and cast their ballots in the presidential election. For the first time since the founding of the republic, women participated. They came out by the thousands and took their places as full-fledged citizens on a par with men—at least in the voting booths.

That same day, another historic "first" took place in a cramped and cluttered shack atop a roof near East Pittsburgh, Pennsylvania. The unimposing shed held a jumble of wires, dials, switches and coils. It was the pioneer radio broadcasting station in the United States—Station KDKA owned and operated by the Westinghouse Company.

On November 2, the station broadcast the election results. Only a few "wireless bugs," hobbyists, who had built their own crude receiving sets heard KDKA's transmission and learned that Harding and Coolidge had swamped Cox and Roosevelt by 16,000,000 votes to 9,000,000. The rest of the country did not find out the election results until the following day when the first editions carried the news.

The significance of the broadcast which heralded a new era in communications was lost on the American public and attracted scant notice in the press. One cynical newsman shrugged off the KDKA experiment by writing: "This radio or wireless telephony or what-you-may-call-it isn't even worthy of discussion. It's a toy, a fad, a gadget. Nobody cares now and nobody will remember it in a year. . . ."

At first radio broadcasting made only slight headway but it continued on an experimental basis. New stations opened. Technicians learned how to muffle outside noises so that music could be sent over the airwaves. By the winter of 1921, a San Francisco journalist could write, "There is radio music in the air, every night, everywhere. Anybody can hear it at home on a receiving set which any boy can put up in an hour."

Radio caught hold in the U.S.A. soon afterwards. Within a year, Americans spent $60,000,000 on radio sets, parts and accessories. In less than ten years that figure soared to more than $800,000,000 a year and one out of every three homes in the United States had some sort of radio receiver.

No one could tally the millions of radio fans who spent numberless hours twiddling the dials to hear a dance band eight hundred miles away playing a popular tune.

"I got Dayton, last night," a New Yorker boasted at the office. "Came in clear as a bell. My radio set's a lulu!"

Thus, on November 2, 1920, the United States once again was poised on a threshold: radio foreshadowed the Age of Electronics, the world of the future. Yet, Warren Harding spoke of the return to "normalcy," a clinging to the past. He declared: "America's present need is not heroics but healings; not nostrums but normalcy; not revolution but restoration . . . not surgery but serenity. . . ."

In Warren G. Harding, the voters had chosen a man diametrically opposed to Wilson in viewpoint, concept, intellect and personality. Wilson was a progressive while Harding linked himself with the past. As one observer remarked of him: "Warren Harding is as old-fashioned as a wooden cigarstore Indian."

Wilson was cold and withdrawn; Harding, warm and friendly. Wilson, who had favored labor unions, also distrusted businessmen as a class and advocated strong governmental controls over them. Harding, on the other hand, yearned for the good old days when Uncle Sam left businessmen alone and never bothered them with "unnecessary" regulations. He had no use for trade unionism and looked upon labor leaders with suspicion. Harding's labor relations credo was "a fair day's work for a fair day's pay," without spelling out what he meant by "fair."

Wilson was an internationalist. Harding stood for America first. He demanded little from the American people and unlike Wilson did not ask the nation to exert itself on behalf of the world's downtrodden masses. What Warren Harding wanted was for the U.S.A. to mind its own business and "get to work keeping shop," as he put it in his folksy language.

After voting Harding into office, the average American might have reasoned this way: "Well, now we're through saving the world and butting in where we don't belong. This new man has common sense and down-to-earth ideas. He's no highfalutin dreamer. Now we'll go places!"

Yet the ordinary citizen was not quite satisfied. Somehow, a sliver of doubt remained in his mind. How could he be sure that Harding's isolationism was better for the country

51

than Wilson's internationalism? Had the slogan "Make the world safe for democracy!" been a sham and a fraud? If so, had all those boys in the United States military cemeteries sacrificed their young lives for nothing at all?

That was hard to believe and even harder to accept. So the average American was apprehensive as he awaited Harding's "Reign of Normalcy." And he was worried, too. What if Harding's way did not turn out to be an abiding blessing? After all, in such volatile times who could define the "normalcy" to which the handsome senator from Ohio had pledged a return?

☞ 4

"They're running wild!"

The Harding "Reign of Normalcy" started March 4, 1921, when Woodrow Wilson limped out of the White House to the privacy of a brooding retirement. With Wilson gone, good will and affability ruled the White House. But anyone with the keenness to see through all the hand-clasping and back-slapping that replaced Wilson's aloofness might have been disturbed about the future.

Warren G. Harding was the product of a corrupt political machine. Ohio politics were notoriously dirty. While Harding was personally honest, he had always gone along with the machine that lifted him from the editorship of a newspaper in Marion, Ohio, to the United States Senate and then the White House. He was suited neither by training nor temperament to hold the top executive position in the country.

When confronted by problems, Harding solved them with a laugh, a compliment or a hearty display of good fellowship. As President he once left a heated debate over a tax issue.

Back in his own office he wearily complained to a secretary: "I can't make heads or tails of it all. First one bunch seems right, then the other. I know somewhere there's a book that'll give me the truth, but I couldn't understand the book. I know somewhere there's an economist who knows the truth, but I don't know where to find him and haven't the sense to trust him if I did! Oh, what a darned job this is!"

Harding's one desire was to act in a neighborly fashion toward all—especially the folks back home in Marion, Ohio, who had helped his campaign. He proved this neighborliness by appointing long-time political friends to key government jobs. For his cabinet, Harding made three intelligent choices: Charles Evans Hughes, Secretary of State; Herbert Hoover, Secretary of Commerce; and Andrew Mellon, Secretary of the Treasury. The rest of his selections ranged from mediocre to poor.

Out of misguided loyalty to undeserving people, Harding surrounded himself with advisers who were dishonest, incompetent—or both. His administration quickly became a pasture for grafters, lobbyists and deal makers. It became a carnival for profiteers and crooked operators as the glad word went out that anyone could do business with the government by greasing the palm of the right man.

Harding's "normalcy" soon became synonymous with bribery, corruption, graft and rascality. But it was to take a while before this rottenness showed through the façade. The public never suspected anything unsavory was taking place in the highest governmental circles, although Albert B. Fall, the Secretary of the Interior, was involved in a conspiracy that rocked the nation a few years later—the Teapot Dome Scandal.

Fall took a large bribe to lease the United States Naval

Oil Reserve land known as Teapot Dome to private speculators who then sold the Navy's oil back to the government at scandalously high prices to make fabulous profits.

Teapot Dome was the biggest swindle carried off behind unsuspecting Harding's back. Every day dozens of little deals were made, contracts for shoddy work approved, there were bribes, kickbacks, cheating, grafting. And all the while Harding smiled, flattered and cajoled his way into the good graces of the American public, a dupe in the hands of vicious and unscrupulous men.

As the first months of his administration slipped by, it became clear that the so-called normalcy resembled no other period in the American past. There had occurred since the war a complete upheaval in the attitudes and behavior patterns of the nation's youth. Girls barely out of their teens wore short skirts, bobbed their hair, smoked cigarettes in public and used cosmetics—things no well-bred girl would have done a few years earlier. This was the day of the "flapper" and her boy friend, the "cake eater."

It was a razz-a-ma-tazz time of hip flasks filled with bootleg "booze." Sporty young men with slicked-down hair danced the Charleston in a thousand roadhouses or parked their roadsters along a thousand dark lanes with bobbed-hair flapper girls.

Folklore has depicted the "Roaring Twenties" as a decade of universal debauchery, high living and wealth for everyone. This was far from the truth. During the twenties at least 10,000,000 American families earned less than $2,000 a year. At the time, economists estimated that sum to be the minimal subsistence level needed by a family of four. Obviously, people with such low wages were not driving fast roadsters or making "whoopee" at all-night gin parties.

However, the American wage earner was better off than ever before and while the United States economy suffered a postwar slump in 1920–1921, it enjoyed a quick and sensational recovery. Jobs became plentiful again and while not everybody was rich, only a handful suffered actual want.

Things looked good in those honeymoon days of the Harding administration. Most people were satisfied with "normalcy," although a few thin-lipped, blue-nose reformers kicked up a fuss about the carryings-on of the younger set.

"They're running wild!" thundered a minister from his Larchmont, New York, pulpit. "I call upon the older generation to check the downfall of our youth by setting an example of decency for them to follow!"

"Nothing to worry about. Those kids are only kicking up their heels," came the rejoinder.

The gin parties, the roaring cars, the outlandishly short flapper skirts, the raccoon coats and untrammeled behavior somehow all seemed to fit the spirit of the times. Instead of curbing their children, parents emulated them. If daughter wore her skirt short and tight, so did mother; if daughter bobbed her hair, so did mother; if daughter smoked and drank in public, so did mother.

A compulsion to "stay young" and "act young" goaded rich and upper middle class adults to behave strangely. It grew commonplace to see paunchy, balding middle-aged men doing the current dance craze, the Charleston, while their portly wives, ungainly and graceless in sleeveless knee-length dresses, puffed cigarettes from long holders in pathetic imitation of the slinking, sultry movie "vamp," Theda Bara.

This illogical drive to evade reality was carried out to the accompaniment of moaning saxophones, clinking glasses, racing motors and high-pitched laughter. Everyone who could

56

afford to do so, enjoyed the endless spree. Americans drank too much, ate too much and spent too much.

The pace was fast and picking up speed on the way. Nobody seemed to worry that a whole social system was traveling on a roller coaster. The ride was destined to be a long and gay one before the cars jumped the tracks.

5

"He's dead, I tell you!"

During his third year in office, President Harding with his wife, physician, several cabinet members and a corps of newsmen, set out late in June 1923 on a junket to Alaska. The President appeared to be troubled and preoccupied when he left Washington. Yet he managed to smile and wave to the crowd that had come to bid him farewell as he boarded his special train.

The people genuinely like the genial Ohioan. There was every reason for him to be popular. Business had never been better. The country was doing fine. So well, in fact, that 16,000,000 Americans owned automobiles. Even poor farmers and slum-dwelling, low-paid factory workers managed to scrape up enough to buy an aged "Tin Lizzie." There were those with cars who lived in houses and tenements without proper bathrooms, which led a foreign observer to remark, "Americans are a funny race—they'd rather ride than bathe."

On the day in June 1923 when Harding left for Alaska, the only discernible cloud in the American sky was the depressed state of farm prices. If industrial workers were somewhat better off than they had been before the war, farmers were distinctly worse off.

During the war years they had increased their acreage under crops to raise food for Europe. There had been a rapid increase in farm prices, land values and the quantity of farm mortgages. When the war ended, farm prices fell sharply because Europe no longer needed American farm products. But the farmer could not afford to let his newly acquired fields lay fallow, so he kept growing corn, wheat, barley and rye, bringing on an overproduction of those commodities.

Individual farmers found it almost impossible to keep operating. Thousands of them left the land for the city factories, and the independent farmer, the stalwart of the American past, began to vanish from the contemporary scene in the 1920's.

An expert predicted that by 1940 "ninety-five per cent of all agriculture in the United States will be controlled by great farming trusts working huge tracts of arable land. . . . The knell has sounded for the family-owned farm. . . ."

Not much federal attention was paid to this problem as the belief spread that the formula for national prosperity was no governmental regulation of private enterprise. "More business in government, less government in business," became the slogan of corporations, industrialists, manufacturers and merchants. Even the owner of the humblest corner grocery store spoke against letting "the fuzzy-minded bunglers in Washington" meddle in the affairs of business. He thus placed himself on the same side with the coal and steel barons, the railroad tycoons and the auto magnates—at least in his own mind.

According to some it all boiled down to the fact that the country needed men with know-how and horse sense—hard-headed, clear-thinking businessmen—to run things. By 1923 they were in full charge and apparently doing a great job. Back in 1920 when government wartime controls were still in effect, there were 4,200,000 unemployed and another 1,000,000 or so on strike. Three years later, with the controls lifted, there were only 1,000,000 unemployed and almost no strikes. Didn't that show what businessmen could accomplish when left to their own resources?

Actually, the prime reason for labor peace in the United States was that by 1923, the American Federation of Labor (AFL) had dropped its postwar militancy. The walkouts and work stoppages of 1919–1920 were all in the past. A resurgent prosperity and Harding's "normalcy" had sapped the labor movement's fighting spirit. Labor leaders now vied with corporation heads as pillars of conservatism. It had become "un-American" to talk of striking—only Red malcontents still thought of strikes as any solution to labor's problems.

Why should labor want to throw a monkey wrench into the wheels of prosperity? Where else but in the U.S.A. did a workingman own a car and eat steak as often as he pleased? Only fools or Bolsheviks would stir up trouble now.

The leaders of the AFL pointed out to grumblers in union ranks that labor conditions had been vastly bettered since the postwar unrest. Of course, they knew some abuses still existed. For instance, thousands of workers were still being paid a bare subsistence wage. In southern textile mills children twelve years of age and younger toiled long hours at the looms. Almost all of the workers in such basic industries as steel and automobiles were unorganized.

Scores of sweatshops, where men and women labored under the worst possible conditions, operated in the fur and garment districts of New York City.

There were many causes for the trade unions to fight if they so chose, but the AFL bureaucrats sat still and did nothing. As one high Federation official said, "You can't have Utopia. This is the U.S.A. not the Garden of Eden. Most of our working people are satisfied. The others are simply out of luck." In other words, "normalcy" and "prosperity" were great for some. The less fortunate had to struggle along as best they could. And so, the United States went merrily on its way without ever pausing to take a long look at itself. A sudden, tragic jolt made the country take notice for a little while. As President Harding was getting ready to come home from Alaska, he was stricken by an illness which his doctor diagnosed as ptomaine poisoning. According to the official version, the President had been felled by a salad with tainted crabmeat on his last night in Alaska.

The sick President was rushed by fast steamer to a hospital in San Francisco, and the anxious country awaited word of his condition. Just when Harding seemed to be recovering, pneumonia set in and he was put back on the danger list. For days he hovered between life and death. Then, on August 2, 1923, a *New York World* reporter traveling with the presidential party called his editor by long-distance telephone.

"How's the President?" the editor asked. The connection became indistinct for a moment and he did not hear the reply.

61

"What? I don't get you," the editor complained.

"He's dead I tell you! He's dead!" the reporter shouted. "They say it was heart failure!"

A shocked nation went into mourning. Thousands of grieving men, women and children gathered along the railroad tracks to watch the train bearing the President's body to Washington rumble by.

From one end of the country to the other, schools and businesses, banks and brokerages suspended operations. All public buildings were draped in black. Flags flew at halfmast. Innumerable speakers eulogized the dead President as a "martyr to duty." Orators called him a "symbol of Christian kindliness and brotherliness." But all their praise could not long conceal the corruption of his closest associates.

Warren Harding had given too much trust to unscrupulous men. They had betrayed him and only belatedly had he learned how he had been used and his high office besmirched.

Reporters on the Alaskan trip revealed that the President was constantly moody and depressed. He worried about the future and expressed his apprehensions freely. Once he turned to Herbert Hoover, his Secretary of Commerce, and asked, "What does a President do whose friends have betrayed him?" Hoover made no reply. There was no answer to that question.

Not long after Harding's death rumors cropped up that he had committed suicide for fear of impeachment and disgrace. Other equally insistent whispers implied he had been murdered by the grafters and corruptors who had been his friends.

The exact cause of Harding's death has remained undetermined and may be a mystery forever. But whether it came through heart failure, suicide or murder, those closest to the President knew the genial man from Ohio had probably welcomed death as the only decent escape from his predicament.

☞ 6

"We're on a rocket to the moon!"

On the afternoon of Tuesday, August 2, 1923, Calvin
Coolidge, Vice-President of the United States, was spending
a few days visiting his father in Plymouth, Vermont. Coolidge's thoughts at the moment were more likely focused on
fishing than national affairs. A slender man with sandy hair,
a sharply pointed nose and a perpetually sour expression, the
Vice-President had been nicknamed "The Yankee Sphinx"
by Washington newsmen because he seldom made public
statements.

Some reporters suggested that Coolidge kept silent because
he had no opinions on anything. Others felt he was playing
it safe by never revealing his position on any issue. Whatever
the reasons for his taciturnity, Coolidge showed that he was
neither a deep nor original thinker in the few statements he
did make. During the business slump of 1921, he remarked:
"When large numbers of men are thrown out of work, unemployment results." This elicited a reporter's comment:

64

"Now I know why he never opens his mouth. He's afraid to put his foot in it."

In spite of his untalkative nature, Coolidge had certain old-fashioned virtues which made him a popular figure for many Americans. He was honest, shrewd and thrifty. These characteristic traits of his native Vermont Coolidge brought to the White House. He was a man without pretensions and never saw himself as a hero storming the ramparts of social reform. In his long public career as the mayor of Northampton, Massachusetts, state senator, lieutenant governor and governor of the state, the only time Coolidge had taken truly decisive action was during the Boston police strike.

However, he served in every post with integrity, honor and competency. Coolidge believed in private enterprise, individual initiative, no government interference with business, and strict economy. The Vice-Presidency of the United States was an ideal job for him. He did it well and unobtrusively. Had President Harding not died in office, Coolidge would probably have faded from the scene into the respectable obscurity which history reserved for most American Vice-Presidents.

But destiny had other plans for Coolidge and they came to pass on that fateful Tuesday in August 1923 when the telephone jangled in his father's modest house and the Vice-President learned his chief was dead.

Within a short time, newsmen and photographers swarmed all over the place. Flash powder flared as Coolidge's father, a justice of the peace, administered the oath which made his son Chief Executive of the United States. The swearing-in ceremony was repeated on August 17 in Washington before Justice A. A. Hoehling of the Supreme Court of the District of Columbia.

Under Coolidge, Harding's crooked friends gradually vanished from the Washington scene. The politicians, grafters and deal makers returned to their own bailiwicks, aware that Coolidge could not be tricked into playing their game.

Harding's "Reign of Normalcy" gave way to a period of business prosperity. The years between 1923 and 1929 became known as the "Era of Coolidge Prosperity." For almost seven years, the nation was literally engulfed by prosperity. More people than ever before had more of everything. No previous generation of Americans had ever lived better.

Many factors accounted for the prosperous years, but the chief cause for the growth of wealth was the increase in the productivity of labor, which was brought about by new mechanical inventions, the development of new sources of power and new manufacturing techniques.

It was widely believed that prosperity would continue indefinitely without any of the periodic depressions which had recurred during the nineteenth century. Forward-looking men were convinced that poverty was steadily being abolished in the United States.

The war, which had devastated Europe, left the United States unscathed. With her modern factory methods that could produce goods in astounding quantities, America soon became the economic master of the world, while prostrate Europe struggled to regain its productive capacity. New products, new methods, wide-open markets and a highflying economy created the great upsurge of American prosperity.

"No nation, no people on earth, has ever attained what we now have," a Republican party spokesman exulted. "It's a modern miracle! An economic marvel! It's a circus! We're on a rocket to the moon!"

It was also a time when a get-rich-quick spirit possessed the

66

country. A building boom started down in Florida, and people scrambled to buy land in Miami, Coral Gables, Daytona Beach and Jacksonville. Land was at a premium everywhere in the Sunshine State. The cry, "Go to Florida!" became as famous as Horace Greeley's advice to "Go West!" Millions of dollars went on harebrained schemes to build resort cities on swampland and mud flats.

By 1924, the Florida Land Rush was on in full cry. But alas for all the dreams of untold wealth! Most developments fizzled out. Too many acres bought by speculators proved to be under several feet of water and impossible to reclaim.

Then in September 1926, a pair of tropical hurricanes barreled into the Miami area and wiped out nearly all the newly constructed coastal communities.

But not even this disastrous setback could stall the forward thrust of Coolidge Prosperity. Business activity doubled, tripled and quadrupled. Office buildings rose in every town and city across the nation. Bright new skyscrapers jutted upward. In New York, towering forty- and fifty-story business cathedrals poked their glittering pinnacles into the skyline, particularly in the Grand Central Terminal district.

New suburbs were created around the edges of cities. They seemed to have been evoked by a magician's wand, so swiftly did they spring up. Tudor houses, Spanish stucco houses, Cape Cod houses of every size and dimension reached out in endless rows as bulldozers, power shovels and pile drivers turned woods and farms into realty developments.

The period was an incredible one. It was a time when 136,000 people paid $2,000,000 to see Gene Tunney fight Jack Dempsey at Philadelphia in September 1926. A year later, 145,000 fans filled Soldiers Field, Chicago, and rang up a record gate of $2,600,000 for the return match between

Dempsey and Tunney. The Chicago crowd was so big that those seated farthest from ringside could not even see the contenders.

Americans went sports-mad during the prosperity years. They worshipped Babe Ruth, the Sultan of Swat, who hit sixty home runs in 1927. A craze for golf, once thought of as a millionaire's sport, led to the building of 5,000 golf courses, and some 2,000,000 players spent $500,000,000 for golfing equipment.

College football games drew audiences of 100,000 every Saturday and collegiate football became big business. In a single season, the Yale Athletic Association sold $1,000,000 worth of tickets and Knute Rockne, the football coach at Notre Dame, was as well known as any movie star or the President of the United States.

It was an era of ballyhoo marked by the rise of the advertising agency, the account executive, the supersalesman and the "hard sell." Companies spent millions to devise new ways of creating public demand for their products. "People must be made to realize they *want* your item," an advertising executive declared. "It is our task to persuade and convince them of their desires."

So well did advertising agencies do their jobs that manufacturers of rayon, cigarettes, refrigerators, cosmetics and electrical appliances could not meet the demand.

American affluence was revealed in the number of telephones installed for private use. Only a few years earlier it had been a mark of wealth and distinction for a home to have a telephone. Now, the home phone was as common as a kitchen sink.

For these reasons, no one doubted that Calvin Coolidge would be overwhelmingly re-elected in 1924, after he had

68

finished out Harding's term. The American people liked prosperity. They wanted to keep on riding the rocket to the moon and thought it a good idea to keep Coolidge at the throttle.

☞ 7

"Man, we've only started!"

One of the mainstays of American prosperity was the astounding success of the automobile industry. The factories that poured out cars at an amazing rate, employed nearly 4,000,000 workers. But in addition to the automobile, at least two other factors—both phenomena of the 1920's—contributed to the fabulous American economic story.

The first was the growth of installment or "time" buying. Frugal Americans of past generations had shuddered at the thought of purchasing anything without having the cash to pay for it. But their children and grandchildren went on a credit buying spree.

Why wait to get that new furniture? Buy it on time! Want a car? It's yours on easy credit terms. A radio? Washing machine? Toaster? You don't need cash. A few dollars down, a few dollars a month and you can have anything. Live big on the installment plan. Don't be old-fashioned and wait until you save the cash to have what you want. Credit terms were easily arranged.

70

Only the wariest people realized that installment buying was a mortgage on the future. "Why look at the gloomy side of things?" the majority asked. That was negative thinking and had no place in booming America. Installment buying, some called it "deferred payment purchases," had many advocates—so many, that during the closing years of the 1920's, at least 15 per cent of all retail sales were on credit and better than $6,000,000,000 was outstanding in "easy installments."

The second factor in the unbroken cycle of prosperity was the previously unequaled spread of speculation on the stock market. The quick money fever did not abate after the Florida real estate boom. People had been bitten by the gambling bug. Lose your shirt in Florida, Mac? So what? Coolidge Prosperity wasn't licked by a long shot. A fellow could still make money fast if he was smart. Where did the rich men put their money? In the stock market, of course! Wall Street! That was the place. Sure, stocks, why not? With any luck you'll be driving a Rolls Royce and living on the Riviera in five years.

Mass speculation turned from Miami's hurricane-splintered palm trees and devastated houses to the solid stone and concrete, the stock tickers and the brokerage houses of Wall Street. No hurricane could wreck Wall Street or demolish the great concrete offices of the world's financial center.

Within a year, thousands of ordinary people, who always had left the stock market to bankers, brokers and financiers, were buying stocks indiscriminately—any stocks that were up for sale—good, bad and indifferent stocks. This influx of investors sent market prices higher. The era of the Bull (High) Market set in. The levels it reached can be judged by what happened to a single stock—Radio Corporation of

71

America zoomed from 85¼ to 495 in less than a year!

Most newcomers to the market were buying stocks on the installment plan—"margin" it was called in brokerage house parlance. This meant the buyer put up in cash with a broker, a percentage—usually 25 per cent—of the stock's market value. The broker reserved the right to demand more margin at any time if necessary.

To carry their margin traders, the brokers borrowed money from banks using the stock as collateral. This built a financial pyramid which stood firm only if prices kept climbing or stayed at a high level.

Should prices tumble, the bankers would have to ask for cash from the brokerage houses to secure the loans. The brokers, in turn, would have to call for more margin from their customers or else sell the clients' stocks to get the required cash. Any customer unable to supply additional margin money within the time specified by the broker—usually a few hours—not only lost his stocks but also all the money he had speculated.

Possibly it was this element of risk which made "playing the market" such a thrilling prospect. Here one had all the excitement of horse racing, dice or cards. A man could gamble in the market without any loss of respectability. "Dabbling in Wall Street" gave one a sense of importance. A man with a few hundred dollars riding on a stock felt himself a colleague of such investment bankers as Thomas Lamont, J. P. Morgan and Charles Mitchell.

In that era of the Bull Market at the peak of Coolidge Prosperity, everyone imagined himself a stock market expert. Even the most casual conversation eventually turned to the market and was frequently colored with "inside" tips on some stock issue or another: "I know for a fact that old J.P.

Morgan's buying a couple of thousand shares. What's good enough for J.P.'s plenty good enough for me." Sometimes the advice varied a bit: "Don't ask me how I know, just listen. I tell you to buy that stock now—while it's low. In a week, she'll shoot up twenty points, maybe even more."

Under usual circumstances, most of the several million Americans playing the stock market were reasonable and levelheaded people. Yet, so great was their drive to get-rich-quick that they developed a blind spot about the perils of what brokers called "peanut" speculation in the stock market.

Sober citizens who should have known better took their life savings and bought wildcat stocks with visions of quick profits. Confidence men fleeced thousands of Americans by selling them worthless stocks. But the victims of crooked stock deals represented only a fraction of the housewives, widows, pensioners, shopkeepers, workers and garage mechanics who made up the hosts of small-fry speculators. Most of them were convinced they had acted shrewdly by putting their money into such corporate giants as the American Telephone and Telegraph Company, General Motors or Radio Corporation of America.

Everything might have worked out well for such people had they purchased the stock outright instead of on margin.

As stocks rose day by day, no one worried about margin. In a Bull Market, it presented no problem. Why concern one's self about a call for added margin when the stocks kept climbing? Every upturn of the market brought stockholders millions of dollars in "paper profits." The more timid buyers sold their holdings on a ten point rise, but the greater number added up their "paper" winnings and not only stayed in the market but bought still more shares on margin at higher prices in expectation of even more spectacular advances.

Everyone was optimistic. When a potential investor asked a leading broker if the Bull Market had reached its zenith, he was told, "Some of these prices will seem ridiculously low in a year. The Bull Market is unlimited. Man, we've only started!"

How could anybody doubt such an informed source?

The financier and industrialist, John J. Raskob, wrote a magazine article entitled, "Everybody Can Be Rich!" The way to wealth, the multimillionaire pointed out, was to save just $15 a month and invest it in a good common stock, allowing the dividends to accumulate. At the end of twenty years, one would have at least $80,000 and an income from the investments of $400 per month. This prospect, Raskob pointed out, depended on stock prices remaining at a Bull Market level, a development he confidently predicted into the foreseeable future.

It was a cinch. Put your money in the market and watch it grow. If you didn't feel like waiting twenty years for wealth but wanted to become rich fast, then go along with a speculative stock. There were plenty of those around. You simply phoned your broker, came up with the required margin and waited.

Everybody was a winner!

At least that's how it seemed during the closing years of the Roaring Twenties when the roller coaster was still climbing and before the rocket to the moon fizzled out.

8

"He made it!"

Prohibition gangsterism flourished all though the years of the Bull Market. In Chicago, Al Capone, a scar-faced hood from Brooklyn, hacked out an empire of crime. His henchmen used machine guns and bombs in desperate gang warfare. Lawlessness took hold in Chicago and other cities. The gun, the bomb and the torch replaced justice and order.

Gangs fought to control the sale of bootleg "booze," and the general American public fostered the criminals by patronizing them. Flouting the Eighteenth Amendment had become a common practice. One was considered smart and sophisticated for having a regular bootlegger who provided a supply of bad whiskey at exorbitant prices. A man's measure of success was his ability to pay for booze from an underworld peddler. The active support of the people themselves kept gangsterism alive and made heroes of Capone and his ilk.

But quite unexpectedly, Americans found an old-fashioned hero with all the ancient virtues of courage, modesty and honesty. He was a diffident young air mail pilot named Charles Augustus Lindbergh. The flier gained public acclaim on May 20, 1927, when he climbed into the cockpit of his monoplane, the *Spirit of St. Louis,* and flew the Atlantic nonstop from Roosevelt Field, Long Island, to Paris, France, for a $25,000 purse offered by a New York hotel owner.

When the news broke that Lindbergh had started on his epochal flight, the heart of the U.S.A. went out to the "Lone Eagle" as he was promptly dubbed by the newspapers. People gathered in churches and synagogues to pray for his safety. They blocked traffic in Times Square to watch the news bulletins flashed on The New York Times Building. Wherever they congregated, in fight arenas, ball parks, restaurants, speakeasies, movies or homes, the talk was of the flier they affectionately called "Lindy."

At last more than thirty hours after he had roared off Roosevelt Field, official word came. "Lucky Lindy" had flown the ocean!

"He made it!" jubilant crowds roared.

Lindy had made it! The U.S.A. had made it!

Despite the adulation and the· honors heaped on him, Lindy remained modest and unassuming. The boyish-looking "Lone Eagle" became the idol of the U.S.A. Streets were named for him; a dance craze bore his name; and no one could keep track of all the babies christened either Charles or Charlene after the hero. For nearly the first time in the hectic era of the Bull Market, Americans looked up from the financial section of the newspapers and took pride in being Americans.

That year, 1927, all sorts of people vied for public acclaim: marathon dancers shuffled on for agonizing hours, endurance foot racers, flagpole sitters, boxers, track stars, tennis champions, ballplayers. A marvel took place in a movie called *The Jazz Singer* in which Al Jolson actually could be heard singing! The silver screen had found a new dimension. The talking picture had arrived.

Somehow, Lindbergh spoiled Americans for heroes of lesser stature than his. Public interest was not again aroused to the pitch it had reached over Lindbergh until Sacco and Vanzetti went to the electric chair. That melancholy event touched the social conscience of Americans, although only briefly.

Henry Ford, the Father of the Assembly Line, caused a greater sensation than a score of Sacco and Vanzetti cases would have aroused as 1927 neared its close.

For a dozen years, Ford's famous Tin Lizzie, the renowned Model T, had been first in the low-priced cars. Now Chevrolet threatened Ford's supremacy in the field. As a result, Ford announced he would terminate all production on the Model T, the Tin Lizzie was to be made obsolete and replaced by a modern car.

Rumors ran high about the new Ford. His publicity people shrewdly played on the public's curiosity until December 2, 1927, when the car was unveiled. The response to the Model A, as the revamped Ford was known, could not have been better. In New York, hundreds of thousands struggled into the Ford showrooms. From coast to coast, crowds massed at Ford dealers and salesmen took orders in a record-breaking volume, so that the Ford plant had to work around the clock to supply the demand.

Within a few weeks, Model A's were swelling the flow of

traffic that crawled for miles every week end as Americans piled into family cars for a spin in the country.

It was not important to them that all roads were always jammed and cars could move only a few feet at a time. Nor did it make any difference that the "country" to which they drove was blighted by ugly billboards, eyesore hot dog stands, gas stations and lunch wagons. Scenery and greenery did not mean as much as good business. More cars on the road proved that business was booming, which in turn brought higher prices on the stock market and bigger paper profits.

After all, did anything else really matter? Certainly it did not in the United States of America in the year 1928.

78

9

"Two cars in every garage..."

In November 1928 an exclusive New York jewelry shop advertised as the perfect gift a pearl necklace with a price tag marked $685,000. That same month, a leading plumbing firm announced its latest line of gold-plated bathroom fittings named "Louis XVI Trianon." "These fixtures are the last word in elegance—and require no polishing," declared the company brochure. A razor blade manufacturer featured "custom-honed" blades at three for fifty cents. Many other signs also indicated an unbroken vista of plenty in the U.S.A. Plans were made to build a $15,000,000 theater-hotel on Broadway.

"We'll have our investment back by 1932," the project's director predicted.

In Manhattan, an apartment house to consist solely of sixteen-room suites with eleven terraces at a $45,000-a-year rental was beyond the blueprint stage. Architects were at work creating a new Waldorf-Astoria Hotel, a "criterion of luxury," to replace the old Waldorf at 34th Street and 5th Avenue. On that site, when the venerable hotel was finally demolished, would rise the world's tallest skyscraper, the 102-story Empire State Building, with offices "above the clouds" and a "mooring mast for dirigibles" on its roof.

A few blocks north, the Chrysler Tower, Radio City and other tall buildings were on architectural drawing boards. Bigger, better, costlier was the spirit of the U.S.A. on Tuesday, November 6, 1928, when Herbert Hoover, the Republican presidential candidate, defeated the Democrat, Alfred E. Smith.

Lost amid the Republican party's election sweep was the victory by Franklin D. Roosevelt in the New York gubernatorial race. His triumphant re-entry into politics after the polio attack was a tribute to FDR's will and determination. But Americans were more concerned with Hoover's campaign promise of "Two cars in every garage and a chicken in every pot" than one man's personal comeback.

In 1928, almost everybody knew America's prosperity was reflected on the stock market. Earlier that year conservative investment brokers began worrying about the ridiculously high prices in the Bull Market. Bank loans to brokers amounted to over $3,000,000,000, and cautious observers fretted because they felt the financial pyramid had grown top-heavy.

"Whatever goes up must come down," they warned.

For the first time since the Bull Market had started its roaring charge upward in 1926, investment advisers claimed that "stocks seem dangerously high and might easily slip." Subscribers to market services were cautioned not to overstay the Bull Market. One posed the question: "Is the process of deflation under way?"

Uncertainty about the future of both the stock market and even prosperity was rising, at least among the experts. Those who made the gloomy predictions were correct in their evaluation of the situation. The financial position of the American economy was precarious.

But the people of the United States, content with the bounties of prosperity, disregarded the counsel of the experts. Instead of pulling away from the stock market, they rushed to buy more stocks on margin.

This brought on a precipitous rise in stock prices which reached unbelievable new highs on March 3, 1928. Leading the advance were General Motors and Radio Corporation of America—the success images of Coolidge Prosperity. Automobiles and radio had come to the fore during the twenties. The potential for these industries was endless, especially in radio where scientific developments were opening new horizons such as television, radio telephones to encircle the globe, radio-controlled planes, radio-guided missiles and other electronic miracles.

The buying wave in the stock market continued for days until Radio Corporation of America stock, which had been selling at 94½ on March 3, reached 138½ by the twelfth and the next day shot up to 160—a 21½ point gain in a single day. The stock had split several times since its high of 495, giving owners of RCA shares almost four for every one they formerly held. This trend went on all through April and May. The market sagged in June, but no one took the setback seriously except those hapless speculators who could not produce margin and lost their stocks.

The stock market had its ups and downs until November 1928, when it rose to an astounding peak after Hoover's election. After that, with only a few insignificant dips, the market

81

kept climbing until September 1929, six months after Hoover's inauguration, when it reached an even greater peak.

That summer of 1929 everyone read Erich Maria Remarque's searing condemnation of war, *All Quiet on the Western Front*. Charles Lindbergh married Anne Morrow. Commander Richard E. Byrd was exploring the Antarctic regions (in November, he flew over the South Pole). Al Capone's gunmen had mowed down seven of their gang rivals in a Chicago garage on St. Valentine's Day. People hummed such song hits as "Sunnyside Up," "Singin' in the Rain," "Am I Blue?" and "Deep Night."

Things were looking up in the U.S.A. in September 1929. Nobody gave any thought to possible trouble except the "doom and gloom" prophets. Americans drove cars, wore expensive clothes, lived extravagantly and spent money freely—that is, if they were not in one of the thousands of families with an annual income of less than $2,000. For those individuals, life was both difficult and unpleasant.

In all the United States, nobody suspected that the era of well-being was nearing its end. On September 3, 1929, the stock market reached the highest point it was destined to attain. From that day on, the roller coaster had no direction in which to go except down.

Middle-class Americans envisioned a land of plenty created by their faith in Wall Street and the stock market.

It was a glorious dream. But the time of awakening was at hand.

☞ 10

"I know of nothing
fundamentally wrong..."

Long before the rocket finally exploded and the roller coaster started its terrifying descent, there had been portents that the Coolidge-Hoover Prosperity band wagon was developing serious trouble. That first week in September 1929 as the market touched the ceiling of its long ascent, there was a sudden and totally inexplicable slump in business that affected even the automobile and radio industries. Producers and sellers of such goods as clothing, furniture and electrical appliances grumbled that things weren't right. Store shelves were laden with an overstock of inventory. Factory warehouses bulged with unshipped products.

Then, the market slipped abruptly in a jarring fall that bruised many small-scale holders of margin stock. That slide was a brief one, and by September 19 most issues had recovered to the former high levels of September 3.

However, something was definitely awry, for the market

did not stay on a steady course. There was a second, more rapid decline during the last week in September. On October 4, stock averages were lower than they had been in years. Some showed enormous losses. United States Steel, for instance, which only a week earlier had been selling at 261¾ stood at 204 on October 4. That same day, American Can was 20 points below its high for 1929—181⅞. General Electric had dropped from 396¼ to 346¼, while Radio Corporation of America plunged all the way to 82½ from 114¾.

By every logic, this downward trend in the stock market should have discouraged further mass speculation. But the carpenters, window cleaners, salesmen, truck drivers, housewives and shopkeepers who comprised the millions playing the market were not so easily dissuaded.

"Now's the time to buy," they reasoned. "We can climb aboard when prices are low. The market'll bounce back just as it's done before."

Brokers were swamped by hordes of bargain-hunting margin buyers. By October 4, bank loans to brokers totaled more than $6,000,000,000. Obviously, the lust for quick money had not yet waned in the U.S.A. Although the business picture was murky and the market unsettled, Americans still had confidence that everything was rosy. They were positive the prosperity Coolidge had entrusted to Hoover was not in jeopardy.

"Why, the U.S.A. is as solid as the Rock of Gibraltar," was the consensus of opinion expressed by the man-in-the-street. So, instead of pulling out, more speculators crowded into the doomed structure. The increased buying of stocks did not halt the market's downward trend. Yet no one sounded a general alarm. On the contrary, even those experts who had been so pessimistic back in February and March of 1928

84

seemed unconcerned about the far more dangerous conditions that existed in October 1929.

There were a few exceptions to this. An investment adviser named Roger Babson, who had been nicknamed "Cassandra" because of his dour predictions, earned wide derision by bluntly stating that stocks were bound to drop sixty to eighty points during October. Several other financiers and bankers also foresaw the makings of a debacle—but their outcries were drowned in a chorus of scornful laughter.

The general public preferred to hear happy pronouncements, such as the words of an eminent Wall Street man who wrote on October 15: ". . . it seems most probable that the stocks have been passing not so much from the strong to the weak as from the smart to the dumb."

Another distinguished financier declared in mid-October: ". . . there does not appear to be as yet much real evidence that the decline in stock prices is likely to forecast a serious recession in general business . . . the conditions which result in business depressions are not present."

On Tuesday, October 22, Charles E. Mitchell, chairman of the National City Bank of New York, upon returning from Europe, confidently told reporters: "I know of nothing fundamentally wrong with the stock market or with the underlying business and credit structures."

The important men of finance had only to glance upward where storm clouds were gathering over Wall Street. They had only to feel the ground trembling beneath them. Everything upon which they had based their lives was soon to be destroyed in an epochal financial catastrophe. But those men were only human. If they saw what was coming, they could not bring themselves to believe it. If they read the signs correctly, they refused to understand them.

The impending disaster was so bewildering and frightening in its scope that the mighty were dulled and paralyzed. What man could admit to himself that his world faced momentary collapse? It was better to shun reality and cling to dreams of security, contentment and the established order. Those Wall Street tycoons might have done well to recall the lines written by the poet John Dryden:

> For those whom God to ruin has
> design'd
> He fits for fate, and first destroys
> their mind.

⌐ 11

"It's the end of everything!"

The deluge came only two days after Charles Mitchell had unequivocally endorsed the health of the stock market. Thursday, October 24, 1929, gained a dubious place in history as the day when the bubble of American delusion and self-deception finally burst.

Black Thursday, they called it.

On that grim day, the Bull Market went into its death throes. The crumbling towers of finance collapsed and buried millions of Americans in the debris and rubble.

For a short time on the preceding Tuesday (October 22) Mitchell's views had seemed valid enough. The morning he had so optimistically stated, "I know of nothing fundamentally wrong . . . ," the market opened briskly and by midmorning many stocks showed gains. But during the afternoon, in the closing hours of the session, all issues lost ground. This development did not cause any upsets. The losses were not serious.

On Wednesday, October 23, traders remained unshaken, believing the market was due to make a spectacular recovery. A torrent of selling orders engulfed the market at its opening. By the time the closing gong rang at 3:00 P.M., stocks had tumbled steeply. More than 6,000,000 shares were exchanged in the most active session yet recorded and the ticker ran 104 minutes late. Losses of fifty leading rail and industrial stocks averaged about eighteen points.

Everyone was now aware that serious trouble faced the stock market. Even the most optimistic looked gloomy. "People around Wall Street wore the expressions of professional mourners," an observer noted. "I didn't see a cheerful face anywhere. Things were in bad shape. One didn't have to be an economist to know the market was very sick."

It was impossible to determine how many margin speculators had been wiped out in Wednesday's trading. But Wall Street operators were notoriously resilient. There was no use griping. A man had to expect to take a "shellacking" on the market once in a while. The only thing to do was to grin and bear it. The brokers and financiers looked hopefully to Thursday's trading. Surely, the bottom had been reached, they argued. Things would be brighter and losses were going to be recouped on Thursday. But for the thousands of ruined speculators, it made little difference what Thursday brought. Nothing could help them.

From the moment trading opened Thursday morning, October 24, it was clear that expectations of any stock market recovery were not to be fulfilled. Right from the outset, prices tumbled at a sickening rate. Before the first hour was over, more stocks had been sold than in most full sessions.

Every telephone call brought orders to sell as frightened stockholders dumped their shares at any price rather than put up additional cash to cover the required margin. Losses climbed into the millions. The credit structure was toppling —dragged down by its own weight.

Prices fell and fell again in that selling blizzard. By eleven o'clock fear gripped the stock exchange and panic swept through the trading pit. Frantic brokers struggled to keep apace with incoming calls. The ticker was an hour behind. Prices chalked on the big board were meaningless. Stocks dropped five and even ten points before harried clerks could chalk in the current price.

Word went out that the market had "busted wide open" and so many selling orders poured in from branch brokerage offices that every telephone and telegraph line leading into the stock exchange was overloaded. Fortunes were lost in minutes and the panic became widespread.

"It's the end of everything," a man in the stock exchange gallery exclaimed as he looked out over the excited throngs of shouting, gesticulating traders on the exchange floor.

For many Americans, it truly was the end of everything. Thousands who had been rich only days earlier were paupers by Thursday afternoon. The agony on the stock exchange floor pointed up the nation's anguish.

An observer remarked: "The sight chilled one's blood. . . . I shall never forget the terrified, contorted faces of those who had just lost their wealth as the market dropped. . . . I saw grown men sobbing like whipped schoolboys. . . . It was awful."

The hardiest Wall Street veteran had never experienced anything to equal the cyclone which struck the stock market that day. Distressed traders pleaded for help as the disaster worsened. Could not something be done to save the market from plummeting into the abyss?

Groups of traders, formed into what were known as investment trusts, had pledged to buy outright large amounts of stock if prices fell too sharply, in order to bolster the market.

Only days earlier many big-time operators had proclaimed their faith in the Bull Market and urged the public to buy more stock as they were themselves doing. The great banks—Chase National, Guaranty Trust Company, Bankers Trust, National City—were supposed to be ready at any time to support a sagging market.

But throughout that grueling Thursday morning session neither the investment trust, big-time operators nor the bankers moved to ease the death agonies of the Bull Market. No one offered to buy stock. In the grip of panic, the cry was, "Sell! Sell! Sell!"

That morning, Charles Mitchell made no glowing statements. He stood at his ticker, ashen with dismay. Not only Mitchell but all the financial giants of Wall Street seemed stunned by the immensity of the holocaust.

At noon, crowds began collecting outside the stock exchange. So many people congregated that adjacent streets were closed to vehicular traffic. The people were orderly, but grim. They stared in silence at the stock exchange building with a solemnity generally seen only at funerals.

At 12:08 P.M., those in the crowd who were more observant than the rest might have noticed Charles Mitchell hurrying into the offices of J. P. Morgan & Company across the street from the exchange. Within minutes, Mitchell was followed by Albert Wiggins of the Chase National Bank, William Potter of the Guaranty Trust Company, Seward Prosser of the Bankers Trust Company and George F. Baker Jr. of the First National Bank.

90

The five bankers had come in response to an emergency call from Thomas W. Lamont, a senior partner of J. P. Morgan & Company. After conferring briefly, the financiers agreed that their companies would each purchase $40,000,-000 worth of stocks in an attempt to halt the selling panic.

Lamont held a press conference when the meeting ended. His first words to the newsmen were a masterpiece of understatement:

"There has been a little distress selling on the stock exchange," Lamont said. A roar of laughter from the reporters interrupted him. He waited for it to subside and continued, "We have held a meeting of the heads of several financial institutions to discuss the situation. . . . We have found that what is happening on the exchange . . . is due to technical conditions of the market . . . and not to any fundamental weakness. . . ."

As the press conference broke up, one reporter remarked, "Oh, brother, now I believe that yarn about Nero fiddling while Rome burned."

When news circulated on the exchange floor that the nation's most influential bankers were meeting, prices steadied. Some even rose a trifle. At 1:30, Richard Whitney, vice-president of the stock exchange, appeared on the floor as the representative of the bankers. Within minutes he bought $30,000,000 worth of assorted stocks. This gesture and the cash from the "bankers' pool" ended the rout of Black Thursday.

"It was the shot in the arm we needed," a weary broker exulted.

By closing time, the market had leveled off to some extent. It had been a frightful day. A trading record of more than 12,000,000 shares was established, and not until seven that

91

evening could the lagging ticker finally catch up with the transactions.

The country quaked in terror. Wild rumors circulated: a score of speculators had committed suicide in the stock exchange. Mobs were rioting in Wall Street, and troops had been rushed to quell the disorder with bayonets and bullets. On and on ran the rumors, each one more fantastic than the last. It was a day that would never be forgotten.

For the time being, the bankers' money had checked the panic, but one didn't have to be a financial expert to realize that the economic foundations of the United States, perhaps of the entire world, had been rocked and shaken.

⌐ 12

"How can this be?"

A well-known newspaper columnist wrote on Friday, October 25: "If a single word can sum up the state of the American people on the morning after Black Thursday, that word is 'crushed.' . . ."

Those who had suffered grievous losses pretended to go about their business as usual on Friday. It was a poor pretense. Any phone call might bring even worse news about the market. Men walked with bowed heads, eyes averted, shoulders slumped. Even schoolchildren were subdued and quiet. The older ones understood what had happened. The youngest wondered why teacher's eyes were red-rimmed as though from crying. Buoyant, bouncing Americans—eternally young, full of verve and laughter—had grown old overnight. The U.S.A. had been jarred by a financial earthquake and the havoc left in its wake was stupendous. Breakfast coffee tasted bitter in many homes that bleak Friday morning. Americans were worried and fearful.

The people had gambled and lost but the game was not quite finished. For two or three days stock market prices remained constant. Perhaps the bottom had been reached, everyone prayed.

President Hoover in a White House statement, declared: ". . . the fundamental business of the country, that is, production and distribution of commodities, is on a sound and prosperous basis. . . ." But his words had no basis in fact.

On Monday, October 28, another panic shattered the stock market. It was Black Thursday all over again.

The chaos in Wall Street on Tuesday, October 29, was beyond credibility. Nothing that had happened before touched the wild scenes at the stock exchange. Stocks depreciated so fast that the White Sewing Machine Company valued at 11½ on Monday, opened at 1 on Tuesday. Huge blocks of shares were dumped. These sales were being made by big traders—the small fry had been swept away days before. Within the first half hour's trading on Tuesday, over 3,000,000 shares were turned over. By noon the total reached 12,000,000. Better than 16,000,000 shares were traded that frenzied day.

The crisis spread to the lesser markets such as the American Stock Exchange and the Commodities Exchange. Stocks collapsed in London, Paris, Berlin and Rome. Despair darkened the great financial centers of the world. European investments were closely linked to American companies by trade and financial ties.

In the United States, the enormity of what was happening had apparently not yet penetrated the minds of public officials and civic leaders. Government dignitaries made encouraging speeches about conditions and predicted an upturn. In New York, the city's mayor, James J. Walker, addressing a luncheon of motion picture exhibitors at the Hotel Astor, offered a solution to the stock market situation. "You people must not show sad pictures. You must show pictures that will encourage folks. All we need to straighten things out is a cheerful outlook. . . ."

But the governing committee of the stock exchange came up with a more practical idea. It was decided to hold only half-day sessions of the stock exchange until the "abnormal conditions that prevail are resolved."

John D. Rockefeller, the oil magnate, spoke up: "I believe the country is sound. . . . There is nothing in the business situation to warrant the destruction of values that has taken place on the exchange. . . . As a result, I have decided to purchase sound common stock . . . and urge the public to do the same."

Unfortunately, the people could no longer afford to follow Mr. Rockefeller's suggestion. Besides, nothing anyone said or did had any beneficial effect. Even with shorter sessions, the stock market slipped lower until November 13, 1929, when it struck bottom.

The fabulous era of the twenties was over. The American dream of affluence and luxurious retirement evaporated. In every town, families that had been living in showy opulence now languished in debt. Those who thought they had reached the top of the long, steep road to riches were back at the foot of it again. The saxophones were stilled. The giddy whirl was done.

The show business newspaper *Variety* summed up the stock market crash in a single headline: WALL STREET LAYS AN EGG!

And what an egg! It had cost the American people $30,-000,000,000. A business magazine described the crash as

". . . the financial catastrophe of all the ages. . . ." Thirty billion dollars! More money than the United States had spent during the World War. More money than all the war debts owed the United States by Europe. All of it lost in the ruins of the Bull Market.

Although the roller coaster lay in twisted wreckage, Americans still clung to the illusion that somehow, despite everything, the golden days of prosperity were not yet ended. President Hoover tried desperately to revive the economy. He called for public works and increased federal spending on government building.

Billboards were placarded with posters showing the country's determination: "All right, Mister—now that the headache's over, LET'S GET TO WORK!" A song copyrighted on November 7, 1929, became a national favorite. It was called "Happy Days Are Here Again!" Everybody sang it just as they repeated the hopeful phrase, "Prosperity is just around the corner!"

But neither the songs, the slogans, nor people's forced confidence could help business. Soon retailers of such luxury items as jewelry, fur coats, expensive cosmetics and perfumes began to close their doors. "Store For Rent" signs appeared on every Main Street. Factories started laying off workmen. Unemployment rose.

"How can this be?" the bewildered people asked.

Prosperity had proven to be a mirage and this was not an easy fact for Americans to accept. Since 1919, accustomed to good living, Americans had created a nice little world for themselves. Now that world had been turned upside down.

There had to be a re-evaluation in the United States—the acceptance of a completely new way of life. The big spree of the twenties was ending in despair. Americans faced with ap-

96

prehension the coming decade. What new disappointments awaited them in the thirties? What new dangers? Fortunately, no man could foresee the future. That was the only solace for the unhappy nation.

III

DECADE OF DESPAIR
AND HOPE

1930–1940

"I see one-third of a nation ill-housed, ill-clad, ill-nourished. It is not in despair that I paint for you that picture. I paint it for you in hope, because the nation, seeing and understanding the injustice in it, proposes to paint it out. . . . The test of our progress is not whether we add to the abundance of those who have much, it is whether we provide enough for those who have too little. . . ."

FRANKLIN D. ROOSEVELT
Second Inaugural Address
March 4, 1937

1

"...everybody is anxious to be at work..."

On New Year's Day, 1930, Andrew W. Mellon, the Secretary of the Treasury, a multimillionaire who controlled the giant Aluminum Company of America and all its many subsidiaries, delivered a radio broadcast to the nation.

Troubled Americans gathered around their receivers to hear the Secretary. The tall, spare, white-haired official spoke with firm conviction as he said:

> I see nothing . . . in the present situation that is either menacing or warrants pessimism. During the winter months there may be some slackness or unemployment . . . but I have every confidence that there will be a revival . . . in the spring and that during the coming year the country will make steady progress. . . .

These were encouraging words to bolster the bewildered American people. If any man knew what he was talking

101

about, that was Andrew Mellon, they reasoned. A sigh of relief rose from all who heard his New Year's message or read the speech in the newspapers. His confident tone was comforting. Perhaps, after all, things weren't as black as they seemed.

Newspaper columnists pointed out that the October 1929 panic had not been the first such crisis the country had ever faced. Back in 1857, 1873 and 1907, the national economy had been shaken similarly by financial debacles followed by depressions. Yet the United States had ridden out each storm and emerged from the ordeals stronger, richer and healthier than ever.

Arthur Brisbane, the most widely syndicated columnist in the country, sounded an optimistic note to his millions of readers. On January 1, 1930, he wrote:

> Now that the "big wind" that swept through Wall Street, blowing away paper profits, has died down, there are sad hearts, but no real losses. . . .

By mid-January even the professed pessimists were persuaded that Brisbane was right and Andrew Mellon a prophet with uncanny powers. For during the second week of the New Year, the stock market stirred in its coffin.

All at once, it experienced a burst of bullish activity. Brokers who had been slumped morosely at their desks perked up as the tickers clattered to record mounting buying orders for all listed issues.

Many experts had predicted an upturn in the stock market ever since the crash, but none expected the swift recovery that was taking place so soon. Prices rose and rose, some even reaching 1929 pre-panic levels. All this came about not through any miraculous recovery of the nation's economy—

102

business still remained sluggish—but because speculators, who still had some resources left, were convinced they had been caught in nothing more serious than a downturn in the business cycle. Having decided this, they felt the time was right to get back into the market while prices were still low. These persistent speculators put together the smashed roller coaster, set it back on the tracks and started off on another uphill ride.

Trading volume equaled the best days of 1929. Prices shot higher. Before long everyone was hailing the Little Bull Market of 1930 and the lyrics of "Happy Days Are Here Again" did not seem so ironical. A wave of premature jubilation was touched off amid lurid predictions that a "new day is dawning" and "prosperity is no longer around the corner but has come back again."

However, the elation on Wall Street brought little response from a majority of the 120,000,000 Americans. For even while the Little Bull Market was bellowing, thousands of numbed, beaten men shuffled on bread lines in a hundred cities. On March 1, Miss Frances Perkins, Industrial Commissioner for New York State, announced that unemployment in the Empire State was worse than it had been since 1914 when labor statistics had first been compiled.

Two days later, more than 100,000 unemployed gathered in New York City's Union Square Park to demand that city, state or federal officials take some steps to relieve the suffering among the jobless. The weather underlined mass misery; it was the severest winter in years. On that chilly March morning, the crowds in Union Square stood peacefully listening to speakers calling for public works to create jobs, increased relief and free hot lunches for schoolchildren.

Suddenly, the demonstration erupted into bloody rioting.

Mounted police charged the throng to break up a proposed march on City Hall, where demonstration leaders had hoped to hand Mayor James J. Walker a petition listing their suggestions for alleviating unemployment.

The fight between police and jobless boiled into a vicious melee. Cars were overturned and set afire. The demonstrators ripped up paving blocks and hurled them at the police. Hundreds were clubbed to the ground—many severely injured. Scores of people were arrested. No such violent disorder had occurred in New York City since the Draft Riots of July 1863.

The New York outbreak was no isolated event. Serious riots flared also in Chicago, Detroit, San Francisco and a dozen other cities as frustrated, desperate unemployed protested their predicament. Many of them were receiving charity from private organizations, which also embittered them.

"We demand work, not handouts!" the jobless chanted.

The press generally smeared the unemployment demonstrations as having been "Red inspired." One leading New York paper editorialized:

. . . the mob of troublemakers that raised all the fuss in Union Square was made up of Communist loafers who wouldn't work if a job was handed to them on a silver platter. . . . Sure, times are tough . . . but any real, honest American workingman who wants a job can find one. . . . This is the U.S.A., not Red Russia! Nobody goes idle here and nobody starves unless he's too lazy to work. . . .

The editorial writer probably knew that the men and women in the unemployment demonstrations were neither Reds nor troublemakers. They were just plain factory work-

104

ers, store clerks, mechanics and seamstresses who could find
no work. In March 1930, there were 4,000,000 jobless,
stumbling from one day to the next, not quite believing what
had happened to them, not willing to realize that society
had no useful place for them. It all made little sense. Gangsters rode in limousines and had penthouse apartments while
decent, hard-working citizens went hungry, were evicted for
non-payment of rent and clubbed by police when they
protested.

Everything was blurred and out of focus in the United
States. All the old values had been turned topsy-turvy, but
the nation's leaders went right on making cheerful speeches
and glowing predictions. On March 3, as New York police
were battling jobless rioters, Secretary of Commerce Robert
P. Lamont delivered a speech to the National Association of
Manufacturers.

"As weather conditions moderate," the Secretary said, "we
are likely to find the country as a whole enjoying its wonted
state of prosperity. Business will be normal in two
months. . . ."

But with the arrival of April and the balmy spring breezes,
business declined further and the Little Bull Market went
to the slaughter pen. During May and June, stocks dropped
to levels even lower than they had been after the 1929 crash.
The end of the Little Bull Market signaled the start of a
long, heartbreaking downtrend in business: a period which
scarred a generation and affected the lives of millions, not
only in the United States but throughout the world as well.

Optimism still prevailed in some quarters. Even after the
Little Bull Market toppled, Henry Ford told a *New York
Herald Tribune* interviewer that he foresaw good tidings in
the near future:

105

Business will be all right. I am not the least concerned. You notice that everybody is anxious to be at work; that is one of the healthiest signs of the times. . . .

It was just the sort of statement which brought forth, in the slang of the day, the cynical retort, "Oh yeah?"

106

⌐ 2

"The country is not in good condition."

Although millions of Americans were feeling the Depression during 1930, it had not yet touched the lives of all.

The wealthy, even those who had dropped a great deal of money in the 1929 crash, tried to shrug off their losses and continued with their golf, cotillions, debutante parties and social activities. Typically American were jokes about the stock market panic and its disastrous aftermath for bankers, brokers and speculators. A popular comedian made this joke famous: "A man comes into a hotel and asks the clerk for a room. So the clerk asks him if it's for sleeping or jumping." The laughter that followed was forced and sometimes a bit pained—but at least it was laughter.

In the country as a whole, most executive jobs were intact. It was only on the lower levels that unemployment was so widespread and to those people who still held well-paying positions the Depression was more of an annoyance than a menace. It was a stumbling block that slowed business and upset the stock market. In one midwestern city, an insurance executive said the Depression was something he "read about in the newspaper." Even though one out of every four factory workers in his city was unemployed, the insurance man's way of life had not yet been affected.

He was no exception. Thousands of upper income men and women never noticed any evidences of the unemployment everyone seemed so concerned about. Their insulated world of security had not yet felt the earthquake—but the shock waves were not to be long in coming, and when they struck, only the strongest of structures would withstand them.

By autumn 1930 the Depression had grown so much worse that even the richest clubman was aware of the problem. That September, the International Apple Shippers Association, finding a huge surplus on hand, hit upon the idea of letting jobless men have the fruit on credit at wholesale prices for resale at five cents an apple. The association's publicity department dredged up the slogan: "Buy an apple a day and eat the Depression away!"

The plan appealed to the unemployed who leaped at the chance to "be in business." Each man felt he was operating on his own and that made him act like a somebody, even though his "business" was peddling apples on the street.

By November, some 6,000 apple sellers were shivering on windy street corners in New York City alone. During the winter of 1930–1931 this number trebled. In Manhattan's busiest districts there were so many apple vendors about that city officials banned them from some streets altogether. Before long, the apple sellers vanished as it grew clear that neither one apple nor ten apples a day could end the Depression.

108

That winter proved a dismal one for an increasing number of Americans. As though unemployment were not enough trouble, added misery fell on the suffering nation. In November 1930, the great brokerage house of Caldwell & Company in Nashville, Tennessee, went bankrupt. This started a chain reaction of failures which brought down 129 banks closely allied with Caldwell & Company. Thousands of depositors lost their savings in the shutdowns.

A short time later, as Christmas bells were tinkling along holiday-festooned Fifth Avenue, yuletide gaiety went out of New York City. The Bank of the United States, with branches in all five boroughs of the city, was ordered closed by state auditors and the bank's officers were arrested for improper use of bank funds. Once again thousands saw their savings disappear.

There were heartbreaking scenes at the branch offices of the Bank of the United States as depositors rushed to withdraw their money when word spread that the bank was going under. Frenzied people milled outside the closed banks, which were guarded by police. A large number of depositors in the bank were immigrants, for the Bank of the United States had three or four branch offices on the lower East Side. A *New York Times* reporter observed at one such office that a policeman, straining to hold back the weeping, pleading men and women, suddenly burst into tears himself.

"These poor people! Every penny gone! Why did it have to happen?" he cried.

No one could answer either the anguished policeman or the many questions that rose on every side. "Why?" the hollow-cheeked jobless asked. "Why?" ruined shopkeepers demanded. "Why?" echoed emptily down all the dark streets,

109

where cold winds froze homeless sleepers huddled in door-ways and chilled ragged, hungry people in bread lines. The country's leaders, the big men, the powerful, the rich had no answers, only banal reassurances. "The worst is over without a doubt," Secretary of Labor James J. Davis had stated in June.

But six months later the jobless, who had numbered 4,000,000 at the beginning of 1930, rose to 9,000,000. Every day thousands of new recruits reluctantly joined what was cynically called The Army of the Unemployed. It was an army without martial music, without uniforms or flags, an army of despair whose sentries slumped on park benches, staring blankly at nothing. The Army of the Unemployed marched with no destination, no purpose and each day that terrible winter its ranks swelled.

As conditions worsened for the working class in the cities, awful privation also pinched many farming regions. In the summer of 1930, the most crippling drought in fifty years gripped the country along the Atlantic seaboard and spread from Virginia and Maryland in a wide belt as far west as Missouri and Arkansas. The sun beat down relentlessly from unclouded skies, and no rain fell for weeks. Crops withered in the fields. Thirst-crazed cattle perished in agony. Wells that had given water for a century went dry.

A wail of grief rose from the stricken land. Farmers watched their cattle die and looked out across parched fields that once had been green with corn, barley, rye and wheat. Now they saw a desert of twisted stalks and cracked, sun-dried earth.

It was a bad time. So bad that when a newsman asked ex-President Coolidge at the year's end what he thought about

110

the situation, the dour Yankee from Vermont shook his head sadly.

"The country is not in good condition," Mr. Coolidge said. "It is not in good condition at all!"

⌐ 3

"I'm afraid, every man
is afraid."

Despite every indication that the nation's most urgent issue in terms of human needs was the rise of unemployment, the prominent men who made up the National Economic League, an influential group devoted to the study of current affairs, when polled on January 1, 1931, as to the "paramount problems of the nation" came up with an odd response. These august gentlemen listed unemployment in eighteenth place behind such matters as law enforcement, prohibition, world peace and other problems. The following year, the League put unemployment and economic stabilization in fourth place after law enforcement, administration of justice and prohibition.

The wealthy, comfortable National Economic League members were more concerned, as one commentator observed, "with moralities rather than actualities. You couldn't

Scene on steps of Capitol, March 4, 1933, as Chief Justice Charles Evans Hughes swears in the new president, Franklin D. Roosevelt. (l. to r. Hughes, FDR, James Roosevelt, Herbert Hoover)

New Yorkers wildly celebrate the Armistice on November 11, 1918

Milling crowds gather in downtown Boston during the unprecedented Boston police strike of 1919

President Woodrow Wilson leaving the Palace of Versailles in France, after signing the Peace Treaty. On his right is Georges Clemenceau, Prime Minister of France; to his left, shaking hands, is David Lloyd George of Great Britain

President Warren G. Harding
on board the *USS Henderson*,
enroute to Alaska in July, 1923

Calvin Coolidge, the outgoing
president, stands beside Herbert Hoover on Inauguration
Day, January 4, 1929

A typical Hooverville on the outskirts of an unidentified city during the early 1930's

Veterans of World War I converge on Washington to demand bonus payments for wartime service

Breadlines such as this were a usual sight in American cities as hungry unemployed gathered to be fed at temporary relief kitchens

Grim-faced depositors anxiously wait to withdraw their savings from a bank in Cleveland during the run on banks

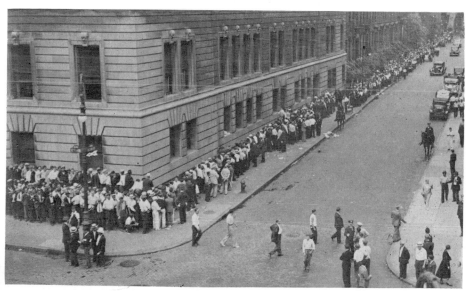

Hundreds of jobless wait outside a New York hospital to apply for a few available low-paid jobs, at the height of the depression

With all their worldly goods and their children crammed into bursting-at-the-seams cars, itinerant farmers crowd the roads, seeking work

Okies live in tents, haul their own water and firewood and eke out a miserable existence during the depression years

To keep warm, Okies paper
the cracked walls of their
shacks with newspapers, calen-
dars and mail-order catalogs

Father Coughlin hammers home a point at a "Social Justice" rally in St. Louis

Senator Huey Long of Louisiana in a characteristic pose as he delivers a rabble-rousing radio address in support of his "Share the Wealth" plan

In Chicago, WPA workers protest pay cuts and attacks on Roosevelt's job programs

Clouds of gun smoke and tear gas obscure fleeing Republic Steel strikers as company guards and police brutally attack c mass meeting

Marchers demonstrate outside the Hershey, Pennsylvania, factory where workers are on a sit-down strike

CCC boys hard at work in a burned-out forest, preparing for the planting of new trees

Storekeeper proudly displays NRA emblem, symbolizing a giant step in combating the depression

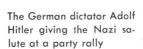

The German dictator Adolf Hitler giving the Nazi salute at a party rally

Benito Mussolini hails a Fascist gathering in Turin, Italy, shortly before the outbreak of World War II

Lieutenant General Hideki Tojo, wartime Premier of Japan, broadcasts an announcement after the Japanese attack on Pearl Harbor

make a mistake by being against crime and sin, but if you brought up unemployment, somebody might ask for a solution to it, and the boys of the National Economic League simply didn't have the answers."

Actually, crime was a major issue in the United States during the thirties. Seldom had any nation experienced such disregard for law and order. New York and Chicago were virtual battlefields as rival gangsters fought to control the liquor racket in these cities. Since everyone was against crime, it proved a safe topic for politicians and civic leaders to deplore. Apparently the National Economic League bigwigs felt it wiser to worry about crime rather than unemployment; it was possible to do something about prohibition and gangsters—but unemployment?

The widespread breakdown of law and order vexed many citizens. Officials admitted it to be beyond control. In New York City, the district attorney frankly stated: "Racketeers have their hands in everything from the cradle to the grave—from babies' milk to funeral coaches."

Although the connection between organized crime and prohibition was an obvious one, the administration persisted in the hopeless attempt to enforce the Eighteenth Amendment. But since nearly every American broke the law, gangsters and racketeers flourished and criminal syndicates raked in billions of dollars.

The federal government foolishly poured millions into its vain efforts to salvage the unworkable amendment, yet refused federal funds for the relief of its starving unemployed. It was all somewhat unreal and somewhat mad. "Malice in Blunderland," a columnist labeled the administration's policies.

President Hoover continued to oppose any federal relief

benefits to the unemployed. He saw such a step as a socialistic threat to the national budget, the self-reliance of the American people and the traditional policy of local self-rule and responsibility for charity and welfare.

Mr. Hoover strongly advocated "rugged individualism" and "self-help." To him, this was the American way. He did relent to the extent of setting up a federal committee to oversee and coordinate unemployment relief. The purpose of this body was not to hand out federal funds but to encourage state and local efforts for charity drives and appropriations to assist the jobless.

Hoover became the target of open abuse because of his position on federal relief. As one critic pointed out, the President had recommended a large appropriation from Congress to lend drought-stricken farmers money for the purpose of "purchasing feed for their animals."

"We have a paradox sitting in the White House," the administration foe snapped. "He's willing enough to spend money to feed hogs but won't let loose a penny to feed hungry people!"

The President defended himself and answered his detractors as best he could. In a statement to the press, he said:

This is not an issue . . . as to whether people shall go hungry or cold in the United States. . . . It is solely a question of the best method by which hunger and cold shall be prevented. . . . I do not feel I should be charged with lack of human sympathy for those who suffer. . . . I am willing to pledge myself that . . . if the time should ever come that the local and state governments are unable to find resources with which to prevent hunger and suffering . . . I will ask the aid of the federal government. . . . I have faith in the American people that such a day will never come.

114

Herbert Hoover was convinced that he was following the right path. But an Arkansas farmer who could get federal money to feed his livestock and not his children, might well have wondered about the soundness of the President's reasoning. The unemployed and the ruined farmers regarded Hoover's tributes to self-reliance with bitterness.

"Sure, we'd like to help ourselves. We'd prefer it!" an unemployed steelworker's wife said. "But how can we? My husband hasn't had a job since early last year. Can't the President see that people like us have reached the end of the line? What's to become of us? Doesn't anyone care?"

So much was going wrong at the same time, that a single housewife's lament was drowned in the chorus of unhappiness. Business was being strangled not only in the United States but all through Europe, as well. The traditional citadels of commerce were toppling. In Vienna, Austria, the most important bank collapsed, and since German industry was involved in the bank's dealings, a terrible panic swept Germany.

The democratic government of Germany, the Weimar Republic, teetered on the brink of ruin as Adolf Hitler led his Nazis in a bid for power. All through Germany, Hitler's brown-shirted Storm Troopers provoked antigovernment riots. The moment of truth was nearing in the Reich.

Elsewhere, the dry rot of Depression was crippling the great, free nations of Europe, especially America's closest allies, Britain and France. In fact, all the democracies of the world seemed to be crumbling, while in the east, Soviet Russia was apparently thriving under its so-called Five-Year Plan, a scientific economic program of production planned to meet the needs of that Communist state.

Soviet-style economy conflicted sharply with that of a free

society, but in depression-ridden lands people started wondering whether it was possible that Russia had found the answer to economic well-being, that perhaps the system founded by Karl Marx and established by Lenin and Stalin might be better than democracy.

It mattered little to a jobless man that Russians were enslaved by Communist dogma and had no political freedom. Freedom was intangible when his wife and children were hungry and he could not pay his rent.

Although the Communist party made inroads among the masses of Europe, few Americans were inclined to embrace Marxism, Leninism and Stalinism. The Reds worked hard to gain American support, but the principles of Washington, Jefferson, Jackson and Lincoln were too strongly ingrained in the American people. It would take more than hard times to wean them away from traditions of freedom and love of liberty.

Despite the suffering, the bitterness and the disillusionment engendered by the Depression, despite the shrewdest Communist propaganda, Americans were not deluded into the Marxist camp. They still preferred the melody of "The Star-Spangled Banner" to that of "The Internationale," the Soviet anthem.

Early in the Depression, there were acts of violence in the United States, of which at least one bordered on insurrection. This was during July 1931 when mobs of starving farmers in Arkansas raided food stores and warehouses in a number of communities. It took the National Guard to end the depredations.

Later that year, thousands of unemployed auto workers paraded outside the Ford plant at Dearborn, Michigan. A trigger-happy guard opened fire on the marchers with a submachine gun and killed four men.

President Hoover met with business leaders and labor chiefs. Bulletins, pronouncements and orders flowed from the White House, but Hoover was either unwilling or unable to understand that only a drastic break with the conservative past could save the nation and that nothing he or his advisers suggested or did could diminish the fury of the Depression.

By the summer of 1931, New York, Chicago, Philadelphia, Detroit and Boston were almost bankrupt and could no longer meet relief payments to their hordes of unemployed. For the first time in its history, Chicago defaulted on salaries to teachers, firemen and police. New York, the commercial hub of the world, had to borrow money to pay its employees.

That summer, thousands of unemployed men, some with families, were living in scrap lumber shacks and shanties on vacant lots at the edges of most cities. These squatter colonies were called "Hoovervilles." In New York City, Hoovervilles sprawled along the East River and on the banks of the Hudson within sight of the fine apartments and town houses that lined Riverside Drive. An abandoned reservoir in the middle of Central Park served as a camp site for hundreds of miserable huts in which people lived as though in the heart of a wilderness rather than a magnificent modern city.

As conditions deteriorated, a reporter for the *New York Herald Tribune* counted more than 2,000 men and women in a bread line on a single block. "The pitiful column of hungry, dispirited people stretched in solid, melancholy ranks along the Bowery for a distance of six or seven blocks," he wrote.

Another journalist, describing conditions in a Pennsyl-

117

vania mining town during the autumn of 1931, said: ". . . the unemployed, evicted from company-owned houses, were huddled on the mountain sides, crowded three and four families together in one-room shacks . . . living on dandelions and wild weed roots. . . . Half of them were sick . . . many were dying . . . and medical treatment was not available."

A Chicago newspaperwoman wrote: "One vivid, gruesome moment of those dark days, we shall never forget. . . . We saw a crowd of some fifty men fighting over a barrel of garbage which had been set outside the back door of a restaurant. American citizens fighting for scraps of food like animals!"

In 1931, anyone with a job below executive level worked at coolie wages. Big department stores paid salesclerks as little as five to ten dollars a week; one New York store would hire only college graduates at those salaries. Factory workers got twenty-five cents an hour, sometimes even less. Topnotch secretaries who had once been paid fifty dollars and more a week were receiving ten dollars. Servants were clamoring for jobs at ten dollars a month including board. Even high-ranking executives had to take substantial pay cuts.

The professional class was hard-hit. Although work still went forward on the Waldorf-Astoria Hotel, the Empire State Building, the Chrysler Tower and Rockefeller Center, construction in New York and elsewhere was practically at a standstill. Architects were doing less than one-seventh of the business they had enjoyed in 1929. Doctors, lawyers, chemists, engineers and other professionals reported earnings at 38 per cent of the 1929 level.

The defenders of the old order, the champions of self-help and rugged individualism were confused and frightened.

Once these men—bankers, financiers, industrialists, government officials, corporation heads—had considered themselves the masters of any situation. They had power, influence, prestige and knowledge. But now, being only mortal, they cowered in fear, hapless men trapped in a raging storm.

A prominent banker brokenly admitted: "You ask me about the causes of the Depression . . . I must tell you that I don't know . . . nor do I know the way out of it. . . . I am lost, floundering, drowning. . . . Why, any shoeshine boy knows as much about it as I do."

One of the nation's important men, the steel magnate, Charles M. Schwab, the head of the mammoth Bethlehem Steel Corporation, speaking at a luncheon in Washington, suddenly looked up from his prepared text and cried out to the startled audience: "I'm afraid, every man is afraid. I don't know, we don't know, whether the values we have today are going to be real next month or even tomorrow."

The darkness of the Depression was so deep and impenetrable that even the most resolute and the bravest began to doubt they would ever again see the light of a friendly dawn.

119

☞ 4

"He is no tribune of the people."

The most ruinous effects of the Depression were not the economic disasters, but the human ones. A social observer of the 1930's wrote: "Depression shows man as a senseless cog in a senselessly whirling machine which is beyond human understanding and has ceased to serve any purpose of its own."

It was precisely this sudden comprehension that individuals were merely "cogs" that shattered the morale of the unfortunate people caught in the Depression's undertow. Nothing anyone did to escape seemed to make any difference.

By 1932, more than 14,000,000 workers were unemployed. The gross figure alone was staggering, but such a statistic did not reflect the dismal toll of human misery. Numbers did not mirror the hopeless defeat of a man vainly trudging from factory to factory, office to office in a fruitless search for a job. The cold figure of 14,000,000 could not show the mount-

120

ing fear in a man's heart as he used up the money in his savings account, borrowed on his life insurance, sold his possessions, piece by piece, took loans from friends and relatives until nothing was left to him except his pride. Then that, too, evaporated as he applied for relief, writhing in humiliation.

This was the Depression. Not numbers, not statistics, not graphs or charts. The Depression was the degradation of once proud men. It was bread lines and evictions, little children without toys at Christmas, men with pieces of cardboard inserted in their shoes to cover the worn soles. It was empty shops along formerly busy streets—shops with wryly humorous signs hanging in dusty windows, "Opened by Mistake" or "Busted and Disgusted." The Depression was a town with Main Street deserted at night. Poverty stayed at home. Movie houses which once had capacity audiences every night now ran features for a scattering of patrons. All places of fun and pleasure stood like vast and empty caverns.

It was a time when sick people could not pay for doctors or dentists, when engineers washed dishes and architects drove taxicabs. No one thought it odd that the usher at a movie house was an honor student in chemistry, recently graduated from a university. It was a time that was best expressed in the words of a popular song, "Brother, Can You Spare a Dime?"

Probably the Depression's cruelest blows fell on the nation's youth. Eager young people could find no foothold for a start in life. The disillusioned Depression generation—the "Lost Generation," sociologists called it—faced the world with despair rather than hope. Some stayed on in school as long as possible, thus postponing the time for coming to grips with desolate reality. There were few jobs to tempt potential drop-outs. Those college graduates who could afford the tuition went on to graduate school—a continuing education was preferable to a vain attempt to begin a career.

The Depression was a fungus that ate away the roots and the morale of the young. All could not stay in school; most could not afford to do so. As a result, thousands of teen-agers and youths in their early twenties took to the road. In an endless, aimless search they hitchhiked from state to state, rode freight trains or just walked. It made no difference whether it was New York, Kansas, Minnesota or Colorado— the answer was always the same, "Nothing doing. Keep moving."

By mid-1932, conservative estimates showed that nearly 500,000 young men and women, many of them in their early teens, were drifting about the country in a reluctant, restless mass migration.

To be jobless for a week, a month, even several months was unpleasant but bearable. To remain unemployed a year, two years, three years was unendurable. Many of those in the dreary lines that stretched before municipal soup kitchens had not worked since 1929. Such idleness corroded thinking, robbed self-confidence and shattered initiative. Some would never again be able to resume useful lives.

No one could measure the extent of human wreckage wrought by the Depression. Marriages were fewer; the birth rate declined; and, in the United States, the suicide rate among male adults quadrupled.

Evicted families moved in with relatives; married children came home to their parents. Sometimes, as many as a dozen people shared a three- or four-room apartment. Meat was regarded as a luxury and served only once a week in many homes, if it appeared on the table at all.

The national diet deteriorated so drastically that the

Surgeon General's office grew concerned about the country's health. A survey made in 1932 indicated that almost 33 per cent of the American people subsisted on an inadequate diet.

That year, 1932, was one of unrelenting and successive misfortunes. Bankruptcies increased daily. Production fell more than 50 per cent in major industries. The prices of commodities and produce went lower and lower while the stock market stood at prices that made the 1929 post-panic values fantastically high in comparison. For example, Radio Corporation of America stock which had fallen to 26 in November 1929 had sunk to 2½ per share!

Despite the clutch of the Depression, millions of Americans who were still employed or ran small businesses strove to retain a degree of normalcy. They curtailed luxuries, put off buying new furniture or a new car, made last year's dress or suit do and cut down on recreational activities. In 1932, a brief Sunday outing in the four-year-old family car was considered the high spot of the week.

A housewife had to shop carefully with her limited budget, and there were bargains galore at the chain store market. A glance at 1932 prices shows that pork loins were selling for 10¢ a pound; filet of haddock was 19¢; oysters brought 17¢ a dozen; salmon steak, 17¢ a pound; cooking apples, 5¢ a pound and one could buy twenty oranges for 25¢.

The daily newspapers ran budget menus which featured dinners to feed four persons at a cost of less than $1. Typical was this meal for 80¢: Roast pork loin with applesauce (35¢); mashed potatoes (6¢); boiled sauerkraut (8¢); bread and butter (7¢); chocolate prune pudding with cream (19¢) and coffee (5¢).

First-rate clothing stores advertised men's suits at a range between $15 and $20 and top-quality overcoats at $20 to $25.

Men's shoes were $4–$6 per pair for the best name brands. Women's clothing ran in similar price categories and children's suits or dresses could be purchased for less than $5.

Apartment rentals even for modest incomes were plentiful. A decent four-room flat in a respectable neighborhood could be rented at $30 a month including steam heat and hot water. For those who had the money, a $65 monthly rental secured a five-room duplex, Frigidaire, fireplace, garage and "beautiful grounds" in Jackson Heights, Queens, according to an advertisement in *The New York Times* that ran during the summer of 1932.

New York City movie houses, featuring lavish stage shows and headline performers, charged 35¢ for tickets before 1:00 P.M. and 55¢ until closing time except on Saturdays, Sundays and holidays, when the price went to 55¢ before 1:00 P.M. and 75¢ after that hour.

Yet, the cancer of Depression had spread so widely that even at those reasonable rates the theaters were seldom filled. Restaurants were offering meals at 60¢ with the incentive for customers to "eat all they wanted" without extra cost. The better-class restaurants provided a full dinner, a dance band and a floor show for $1.50 a person.

But to the jobless, existing in unrelieved misery, none of this mattered. They plodded from one gray day to the next, without comfort or solace. Yet not even the squalid grimness of the Depression could keep the American people from reacting to a personal tragedy greater than their own. On March 1, 1932, the nation was shocked to learn that the infant son of the still shining hero, Charles Lindbergh, had been kidnaped from the flier's home in Hopewell, New Jersey.

Once again Lindy was in the limelight as millions of

people waited for news of the child's fate. After lengthy and complicated negotiations with the kidnaper, Lindbergh paid a $50,000 ransom through an intermediary—but his son was not returned. Instead, the child was found lifeless in a clump of woods about five miles from the Lone Eagle's home.

In an era rife with crime the nation was shaken by the boy's death. Even gangland chiefs expressed indignation over the brutal affair. Every law enforcement agency from local police to the F.B.I. hunted the kidnaper. (It was to take twenty-eight months before he was caught. On September 19, 1934, Bruno Richard Hauptmann, a German-born carpenter, illegally in the United States, was arrested for kidnaping and murder. The evidence against him was irrefutable. He was pronounced guilty and died in the electric chair on April 3, 1936.)

However, the Lindbergh case was only one ugly incident in a disastrous year. The already murky international financial scene was further darkened by the suicide of Ivar Krueger, a Swedish industrialist known as "The Match King" because he held a monopoly on manufacturing matches in Sweden. Krueger was the founder of an investment corporation into which Americans had poured over $250,000,000. When it was discovered that his manipulations were fraudulent, Krueger evaded prosecution by killing himself.

Krueger's chicanery had widespread repercussions. Many banks and other financial institutions were closely involved in his shady dealings and a number of them collapsed as an aftermath of his duplicity.

A few weeks later came another catastrophe. Several thousand American investors—not speculators—who had placed their money into what had been termed "the world's safest investment," were stunned to learn they had lost every penny.

125

The "safest investment" had been a pyramid of public utilities holding companies operated by Samuel Insull, a shrewd Chicago manipulator, whose reputation as a financial wizard had gained for him the faith and trust of the American public.

Insull had formed a complex corporate empire of interlocking companies, but his cold-blooded greed for profits brought on insolvency and millions of dollars were bilked from helpless and unsuspecting persons. Insull's agents had specifically solicited business from pensioners, widows and aged people looking for a "safe investment."

Voices rose above the frightened clamor in this dark time—strident voices of men offering leadership and a "way out." Some were demagogues seeking power; some were decent men who honestly felt they had a workable program to save the nation. And there were also the voices of Communists, Socialists, anarchists and a dozen other radical movements speaking up for a Soviet-style workers' state and the overthrow of the capitalist system.

There were raucous Fascistic voices such as that of William Dudley Pelley, an admirer of Adolf Hitler and the Nazis. Pelley led an organization called the Silver Shirts. His announced intention was to forcibly seize control in the United States, liquidate "Jews, Masons, Catholics, Negroes and international bankers" and "put things right," just as Hitler would soon do in Germany.

Prominent among the voices of Fascism was that of Father Charles Coughlin, the parish priest at the Shrine of the Little Flower in Royal Oak, Michigan, advocating a movement he called "Social Justice." He won a wide following through weekly radio broadcasts in which he lambasted Wall Street, Marxists, bankers and what Coughlin termed the "international Jewish conspiracy." When he openly began to espouse

Nazi policies, the oratorical priest was silenced by the hierarchy of the Catholic Church.

Down in Louisiana, one heard the roaring of bull-voiced Senator Huey Long, who called himself "The Kingfish." A wily, ruthless rabble-rouser, Long ran the Louisiana political machine with the iron hand of a dictator. He gained popularity, not only in his native state, but nationally as well, by his plan for a redistribution of capital in the United States.

"Share the wealth!" Long ranted. "Every man a king!"

According to him, if wealth were properly distributed in the nation, every American man, woman and child would get $5,000 annually. It was not strange that he could attract masses to his scheme in a period when $5, let alone $5,000, was considered a lot of money.

There were other voices calling in the wilderness of the Depression. A retired physician, Dr. Francis E. Townsend of Long Beach, California, was so moved by the sight of three old women scavenging for food in a garbage can that he gave up medicine to become a political crusader. He evolved a pension plan for all past the age of sixty. It called for monthly payments to them of $200 which would be raised through a national sales tax. The only condition attached to the pension was that the monthly check had to be spent at once to put money in circulation. According to Townsend this activity would quickly restore prosperity. Although experts denounced Townsend's plan as unworkable and impracticable, hundreds of thousands of elder citizens signed petitions in its favor and formed lobby groups to pressure Congress into passing such a measure. Townsend Pension Clubs were formed in many states, and while the Townsendites never gained their ends, they were for a time a potent political force.

127

Of all the voices mingling in the Depression wasteland, one in particular evoked confidence and reassurance. That was the voice of New York's governor, Franklin Delano Roosevelt. In July 1932, he was making a bid to capture the nomination as the Democratic candidate for the Presidency in the November election. That July, the Democrats were convening in Chicago to pick a slate. Roosevelt's campaign rested in the hands of James Farley and Louis Howe, two old and trusted friends. His chances seemed good. The delegates—and the American public—liked what he was saying about a New Deal for "the forgotten man at the bottom of the economic pyramid."

His proposals for "persistent experimentation" in government stirred up a great deal of opposition in his own party and among the wealthy classes of the United States. The politicians feared him as a troublemaker who wanted to upset the machine; the rich were afraid that Roosevelt was socialistic or even worse. At least one millionaire financier labeled him a "traitor to his own class" and a "toady of labor." Among those who disapproved of FDR and regarded his support of the downtrodden with disbelief and derision was the widely read, nationally syndicated columnist of the *New York Herald Tribune,* Walter Lippmann. He scornfully wrote:

> Franklin D. Roosevelt is an amiable man with many philanthropic impulses . . . but he is not a dangerous enemy of anything. . . . He is too eager to please. . . . Franklin D. Roosevelt is no crusader. . . . He is no tribune of the people. He is no enemy of entrenched privilege. He is a pleasant man who, without any important qualifications for the office, would very much like to be President.

Lippmann, a distinguished and usually astute journalist, rarely erred in his judgment of people and events. But he was mistaken in his estimation of FDR. Contrary to the opinions of his detractors, Roosevelt was a crusader, a tribune of the people, and an enemy of entrenched privilege as the nation and the world were soon to learn. After hectic sessions on the convention floor, the delegates nominated Roosevelt for President on the fourth ballot.

With his running mate, John Nance Garner, standing on the platform beside him, FDR promised the cheering delegates that he intended to give the country a New Deal and that he meant what he said. The anti-Roosevelt skeptics listened and scoffed. "FDR's getting a bit ahead of himself," they sneered. "He hasn't even won the election and already he's promising to turn things inside out, patch up our troubles and put the country on an even keel. Well, promises are cheap. Let's see what happens if he gets elected."

5

"I'm ashamed of the uniform..."

A few weeks before the Democrats chose Roosevelt and Garner, the Republicans had renominated Herbert Hoover and Charles Curtis as standard bearers of the GOP. Because of the country's plight, Hoover had a slim enough chance to take the election. As though to point up the terrible economic conditions, Hoover received the nomination in Chicago at a time when forty of the city's banks failed within a few days of one another. But the Republican party had little choice except to string along with Hoover. His supporters in the party controlled the majority of the convention delegates, and even before the opening gavel, it was a foregone conclusion that Hoover would win the nomination.

The most loyal Republican was pessimistic about the outcome of the November election, although diehards still spoke of victory and clung to the hope that the voters would be afraid to take a chance on a new President for fear things might get even worse than they were.

130

However, one hot and humid July day in Washington, Hoover lost what little public support he still had by mishandling a situation and earning for himself the bitterest unpopularity. As a result of his ineptitude, an ugly incident —one of the most unpleasant in American history—took place on July 28, 1932, in the national capital.

It had its roots shortly after the Republican convention, during the unseasonably hot days of June, when a pathetic army invaded Washington. From all over the country, thousands of war veterans converged on the city to pressure Congress for immediate passage and payment of the so-called Soldiers' Bonus which had been promised them ever since 1925.

The ex-doughboys arrived in Washington by truck, battered automobiles, freight cars and on foot. Once in the capital, they set up camp on dreary Anacostia Flats, just outside the city. They built a sprawling Hooverville of shacks, shanties, tents and huts to house several thousand people including women and children; some of the self-styled "Bonus Marchers" had brought along their families.

By the beginning of July, nearly 20,000 veterans were ensconced at the Anacostia encampment and a smaller contingent occupied a group of unused federal buildings situated on Pennsylvania Avenue a few blocks from the Capitol.

This "Bonus Expeditionary Force," which the papers called the veterans, was organized by its leaders on quasi-military lines. There were battalion, regimental and company commanders, platoon and squad leaders. Order was maintained by their own "military police" units. The strictest sanitary and hygiene regulations were firmly enforced. On the whole, the BEF behaved in a quiet and disciplined fashion at all times.

131

The Hoover Administration later charged that many of the marchers were not really veterans but criminals and Communist agitators. This was an untruth. No doubt there were radicals, adventurers, tinhorns and unsavory characters among them—but the majority were bona fide veterans in Washington to exercise their constitutional rights to redress their grievances.

The superintendent of the metropolitan police, General Pelham D. Glassford, regarded the men in this light. He welcomed the Bonus Marchers to Washington, helped establish their encampment and treated them with the courtesy and consideration which he felt the veterans deserved. However, not everyone in Washington looked upon the BEF the same way. Some high government officials regarded with alarm the presence of so many disgruntled men.

The nervous authorities suspiciously and fearfully viewed the picket lines of veterans that paraded around the Capitol day and night as Congress debated the bonus bill. On the evening the measure came to a vote, thousands of ragged marchers congregated in Capitol Square to await the results. The Senate turned down the proposal. No bonus payments were to be forthcoming.

Anxious faces peered from the brightly illuminated Senate wing of the Capitol. A rumor circulated that the veterans were preparing to rush the Senate building and heavily armed police were sped to defend it. But nothing like that developed. When the men of the BEF were told the bad news, they stood in quiet dejection for a few moments. Then, a makeshift band struck up "America." First only a handful started to sing the refrain. Then others joined—more and still more, until the sound of their singing swelled upward in a resounding wave. It was a touching indication of patriotism in a moment of utter frustration and disappointment.

When the song ended, the huge throng silently dispersed. The next morning, hundreds left Washington as they had come, but many lingered on. Perhaps because they had no place else to go. They still held the buildings on Pennsylvania Avenue and stayed in the ramshackle Hooverville of Anacostia Flats. Perhaps they clung to their vigil in the obstinate hope that the senators might yet have a change of heart. But the Senate would not change its mind; that august body had spoken. The BEF pursued a dream.

After a week or two, government officials grew uneasy over the prolonged stay of the BEF. "These ragamuffins cannot remain here indefinitely," a senator said. "They have no business in Washington. They don't belong here."

After some consultation, it was decided to evacuate the veterans who had taken over the Pennsylvania Avenue buildings. The unpleasant task devolved on General Glassford. Against his own feelings, the general mobilized a force of police and on the morning of July 28, 1932, moved to evict the veterans. At first the metropolitan police met no resistance, but at noon, a band of resentful ex-doughboys showered bricks on the policemen. Nightsticks came into play; heads were broken and a serious riot seemed to be in the making.

Fortunately, the trouble quickly subsided, but at two o'clock it flared up again—this time with tragic consequences. A policeman, knocked down by a rock, drew his revolver and opened fire. Before he could be stopped, two Bonus Marchers lay dead. Even this disorder abated, but General Glassford then advised his superiors that if the veterans decided to put up determined resistance, this was no job for the metropolitan police.

"Instead of dragging those boys out of the buildings, I suggest that we throw a cordon around the neighborhood and starve them out. If you don't follow this tactic, you'll need the regular army to flush them out of there," Glassford said.

Word was sent to President Hoover that troops were necessary, and the Chief Executive ordered out units of the regular army under the command of General Douglas MacArthur.

In the late afternoon of that blazing summer day, the embattled ex-doughboys on Pennsylvania Avenue were dumbfounded to see an impressive military array moving against them—four cavalry squadrons, four infantry companies with fixed bayonets, a machine-gun section and several light tanks.

"Hey, guys, they've declared war!" a Bonus Marcher cried.

The arrival of the troops attracted a large crowd of spectators who watched the action from an empty lot across the avenue. General MacArthur, resplendent in whipcord breeches and highly polished cavalry boots, gave an order. The mounted units charged into the veterans. The troopers lashed out left and right with the flat of their sabers, and frightened people ran screaming in every direction. Gasmasked infantrymen hurled tear gas bombs and rushed forward with leveled bayonets.

Amid shouts and cries, the soldiers pushed out the exdoughboys. At some points the veterans turned to fight with sticks and rocks, but could not stand against the gas and the cold steel. With stolid efficiency, the army plodded straight on. MacArthur's men drove into the camp at Anacostia Flats and set it afire. Long after midnight, the Washington sky was reddened by the flames of the burning huts. The wretched Bonus Expeditionary Force was broken up, and the veterans limped away from Washington. MacArthur had fulfilled his mission. No one was killed by the soldiers, but several hundred veterans had been wounded or injured.

"Is that the best our government can give us?" a BEF leader asked. "Tear gas, bayonets, clubs, busted skulls? Is that why we went to France in 'seventeen? All we wanted was what had been promised. All we wanted was a little money to buy food for our wives and kids!"

The nation looked askance at this unhappy incident. Wait until November, people muttered. They would show Hoover at the polls how voters felt about a President who treated veterans like dogs.

Perhaps the attitude of most of the country about the "Battle of Anacostia Flats" was best summed up in the words of a regular army captain as he directed the burning of some shacks in the Anacostia camp.

"I've been a soldier for almost fifteen years," he said. "For the first time since I put it on, I'm ashamed of the uniform I'm wearing."

☞ 6

"We are at the end of our string...."

President Hoover worked vigorously during the 1932 election campaign to salvage the political reputation of the Republican party and to wipe out the unpopularity which had resulted from his unfortunate handling of the Bonus Marchers. He stumped the country, making speeches from the rear platform of his special train, in halls, auditoriums, fair grounds and ball parks. He shook hands, kissed babies, signed autographs, posed for pictures and presented himself to the public as an earnest, straight-talking, sincere, but misunderstood President.

He vehemently denied that his administration had any responsibility for the Depression:

"The roots of this Depression lie in Europe, not America. The collapse of the financial structure overseas has shaken our economy. We are caught in the grip of events beyond our control. But I have taken steps to end the Depression in the United States. Very soon now, the measures will become effective and better days will be upon us."

The skeptical voters were astonished in midsummer when Hoover's rosy predictions appeared to be coming true. The stock market staged a miraculous rally. Fewer banks were failing—almost 6,000 had gone under—because at Hoover's request, Congress had set up the Reconstruction Finance Corporation (RFC) with a fund of $3,500,000,000 to aid distressed banks, insurance companies and similar institutions during emergencies. Now that they were backed by the RFC, many banks which might have gone under remained solvent.

There were other improvements in the economic picture. A few factories which had been working part-time, began full-scale operations again. Automobile sales rose slightly. A ripple of optimism filtered through the gloom. In general, conditions throughout the country were still bad, but at least some dent had been made in the Depression. Its grip had been weakened, if ever so slightly.

Hoover warned that a victory for the Democrats would have an appalling effect and would wipe out all the recent hard-won gains. "The grass will grow in the streets of a hundred cities and weeds will overrun the fields of a million farms. . . ."

He pleaded with the voters to give him another four years in the White House. "Allow me the time to complete our return to Prosperity," he urged.

But no matter what he did or said, Hoover was irrevocably linked in the minds of the American people to the stock market panic, the Depression and the heartless treatment of the Bonus Expeditionary Force. To Americans, he epitomized bread lines, Hoovervilles, starving farmers, evicted workers, roving and homeless young people. Often, his remarks were drowned out by boos, hisses and jeers. At one train stop a large electric light bulb was hurled at him. It exploded with a noise like a bomb and secret servicemen, fearful of an assassination attempt, rushed with drawn revolvers to surround him. Probably never before in the nation's existence had a President been treated with such disrespect.

Roosevelt campaigned under entirely different circumstances. Large and partisan crowds turned out to greet him everywhere. His speeches were well received. They found special favor when he stressed the need for federal aid in relief, unemployment insurance, social security old-age pensions and public work projects. In addition, Roosevelt called for an end to prohibition, "that misguided experiment." But his main attack was along lines of social and economic changes —a New Deal for the nation. FDR insisted that "private economic power is a public trust. . . . Continued enjoyment of that power by any individual or group must depend upon the fulfillment of that trust."

He was ably assisted in his campaign by astute advisers— college professors, economists and lawyers—men whom a facetious reporter had dubbed "The Brain Trust."

There were still plenty of citizens who mistrusted Roosevelt. They viewed his social program with alarm as too radical; his economic policies they considered too extreme. But FDR's smiling confidence won the masses and the carping of his critics was scarcely heard above the applause that rang out for him.

As autumn approached, that twitch of recovery which Hoover had called "a return to Prosperity" was suddenly stilled and the Depression closed in more harshly than before. The continuing hard times made the people passionately want Roosevelt's New Deal. They proved this desire on Election Day in November. Roosevelt carried 42 states— only Connecticut, Delaware, Maine, New Hampshire, Vermont and Pennsylvania went against him. The mandate was clear—the American people were through with Hoover and "rugged individualism."

However, because of the outmoded political arrangements for the inauguration of a new President, Hoover remained in office until March 4, 1933. In the course of that four-month-long period, a terrible banking crisis developed.

For many complicated reasons, but mainly because of inadequate banking regulations and widespread speculation in unsound bonds and unsafe mortgages, hundreds of banks were in serious trouble. The reckless practices which had already been responsible for the bank failures of the past brought on a general banking collapse in February 1933 only three weeks before Hoover's term was to end.

As uncontrolled panic spread, anxious depositors rushed to withdraw funds from foundering banks. The Reconstruction Finance Corporation received so many urgent calls for loans that its capital was soon all but depleted. Nothing could avert the banking debacle that was in the making. A whisper, an unbased rumor, a careless word was enough to start a bank run.

In Newark, New Jersey, a perfectly sound bank was almost put out of business because a crowd had gathered to wait for the doors to open at the start of the business day. An onlooker, noticing the throng, spread the word that there was a run on the bank. Within fifteen minutes police reserves had to be called, so great was the rush of depositors to get their money out.

Withdrawing cash from a bank often placed the money in greater jeopardy than if the savings had been left in the bank. A rash of holdups broke out in New York. During a single day, the Brooklyn, New York, police were notified of a dozen cases in which homeward-bound depositors carrying their life's savings had been assaulted and robbed.

"There's nothing we can do about it," a precinct captain said. "My men can't escort everyone home. All the crooks have to do is watch and see who comes out of the bank and then follow him. It's a mess!"

On February 14, there were so many banks in difficulty in Detroit, Michigan, that the governor of the state decreed an eight-day bank holiday which shut down every bank in Michigan and allowed them time to raise necessary cash.

With all the ferment of the bank situation, a favorable vote by the United States Senate on February 16 to repeal prohibition passed almost without notice. The final doom of the Eighteenth Amendment now rested with the states, since a change in the Constitution and passage of the Twenty-first Amendment (Repeal) needed not only a two-thirds majority in both Senate and House, but also approval by three-quarters of the states. The House had earlier voted to end prohibition, and the advocates of the Eighteenth Amendment knew it was merely a matter of time before their cause was dead. (By December 1933, prohibition had been wiped off the books and the country returned to legal wine, whisky and beer.)

The attention of state and federal officials remained riveted on the Michigan bank situation. Hoover worked ceaselessly, conferring with bankers, industrialists and financiers, in an ardent effort to shore up the buckling banking system. For about ten days, the greatest problems centered in Michigan.

Then, on February 24, the bank plague broke out in Baltimore, Maryland.

Panic spread throughout that state with the speed of a wind-driven prairie fire. Soon every bank in Maryland was sending up distress signals. Armored cars carrying RFC cash sped from bank to bank with funds, trying to meet the clamorous demands of depositors. But as the crisis sharpened, the governor of Maryland ordered a bank holiday. The epidemic spread to Ohio, Indiana, Kentucky and Pennsylvania within the next few days and bank holidays were declared in those states.

While the American economic structure fought to preserve itself, democracy collapsed in Germany. On February 27, Nazi agents in Berlin set fire to the Reichstag. They used this as a pretext for inducing the doddering German president, Paul von Hindenburg, to give Hitler emergency powers in order to cope with a "Red uprising." According to the Nazis, the revolt had been scheduled to start during the Reichstag fire. Von Hindenburg foolishly gave Hitler a free hand and the world was faced with an evil unsurpassed since Barbarian hordes swept across Europe and all but obliterated civilization.

But Americans were not too concerned about Hitler or the Nazis in Germany. They had an overabundance of domestic problems. During the first three days of March 1933, the banking crisis deteriorated even further. On Thursday, March 2, when Franklin D. Roosevelt boarded the train bearing him from New York to Washington for his inauguration, the President-elect was heading into a hurricane that carried the seeds of a national catastrophe.

The banks were vital organs of the national economy, the heart, the very life's blood. A wholesale collapse was under way. What would happen? Was this the end of capitalism in America? What would follow in its wake? Fascism? Communism? Anarchy? Perhaps even FDR was uneasy behind the jaunty front he displayed in public. Perhaps as he pondered the problems of the day, he felt a moment of doubt, a weakening of faith in himself, in the people and the American way of life. He knew that each turn of the locomotive wheels was carrying him closer to the storm center. In about forty-eight hours the burden of steering a safe course for the U.S.A. through the wild seas would devolve upon him.

The decisions he made, the actions he took, might well decide the destiny of the United States for all times. It was an almost unprecedented task for a President. The spectre of economic ruin haunted the country, but that was not the only danger. Resentment and unrest were growing among the people. Anger rumbled ominously in the farming regions. The unemployed were getting restive. The good sense and discipline shown by the American people were nearing the end of restraint. Soon pent-up bitterness might burst like a spring flood and sweep the established order before it.

Franklin D. Roosevelt had to satisfy the disillusioned masses. He had to awaken in them fresh hope. He had to fulfill the promises he had made. And he must not fail.

The day before inauguration, Friday, March 3, the tidal wave of financial misfortune battered at the chief economic centers of the United States—New York City and Chicago. There were runs on every bank in both cities. Crowds struggled at the banks from the nine o'clock opening hour until the three o'clock closing. Several leading New York bankers advised Hoover that they could not continue paying off depositors with depleted cash reserves. The same news

142

came from Chicago and then poured in from all over Illinois and New York State.

While President Hoover and his staff were debating what course to take, Governor Herbert Lehman of New York made a decisive move. Despite the repercussions he knew must follow such a step, Lehman ordered every New York bank closed to stop the flow of money from their coffers. The governor of Illinois followed suit. Other states adopted similar measures.

It was a dismal prospect for Inauguration Day—but FDR had three potent weapons: ideas, courage and faith in the American people.

If Roosevelt was anxious to enter the White House, Herbert Hoover had no reluctance about leaving it. Early in the morning of Inaugural Day, he sat at his desk performing the last routines required of him. His face was ashen. He was worn and haggard. He was aware that he would be blamed for the calamitous events that had occurred during his term. He had tried his best to prevent them, but the methods he used were inadequate and obsolete; even his personal viewpoint was anachronistic.

He did not believe in changes. He was not aware of the coming of a new social order, and he clung to the past. He was neither an innovator nor an experimenter. He had fought the Depression with the old weapons and had failed.

When he had finished his duties that final morning, Hoover looked up at an aide. "We are at the end of our string," he said wearily. "There is nothing more we can do."

143

7

"He's a human dynamo!"

From the moment Franklin Delano Roosevelt gripped the lectern that stood behind the batteries of radio microphones, the American people, the whole world, grew aware that a bold and energetic man now commanded the nation. His clarion defiance of "fear itself—nameless, unreasoning, unjustified terror," had emboldened the dispirited American nation. The people were sick of waiting. They wanted deeds, not promises. FDR himself had had enough of words. He intended to give the people action, decisive, purposeful action.

On Sunday, March 5, only a few hours after the inaugural ball ended, Roosevelt held a brief cabinet meeting and then issued a proclamation which stated in part:

> WHEREAS, There have been heavy and unwarranted withdrawals of gold and currency from our banking institutions for purposes of hoarding and
> WHEREAS, Continuous and extensive speculative activity

144

abroad has resulted in a severe drain on this nation's stocks of gold,

THEREFORE, I, Franklin D. Roosevelt, President of the United States of America, in order to prevent export, hoarding or earmarking of gold and silver coin or bullion or currency do hereby proclaim that from Monday, March 6, 1933, to Monday, March 13, 1933, there shall be maintained a bank holiday.

With a single stroke of his pen, FDR brought to an official halt all the banking transactions of the nation. The bank holiday was promulgated not only to prevent hoarding but also to check on the financial soundness of each bank before permitting it to reopen. The President's proclamation showed that the man in the White House definitely intended to run the country. All other bank closings prior to March 5 had been at state and not federal orders. Now the government was taking a hand—a strong one.

Roosevelt's action sent a brief shudder of dread through the nation. There were cries of alarm and warning that momentous Sunday, but also words of reassurance and support for the President. To those worried that the bank closings would foment riots, disorder and even revolution, an eminent economist, Professor Edwin S. Robinson, declared:

Do you think that when the banks are all shut civilization will fall? On the contrary . . . I predict that when the banks close, everyone will feel relieved. . . . It will be sort of a national holiday . . . there will be general excitement and a feeling of great interest. . . .

Professor Robinson proved to be correct. Although the bank holiday added somewhat to the distress of people already hard-hit, Americans reacted well in the exigency. Now everyone was in the same fix. Butcher, baker, newsdealer, broker, pharmacist—everyone in every walk of life, from tenement slum dweller to Park Avenue millionaire, was caught in the same trap.

The bank holiday found most people without sufficient cash at hand and signs quickly went up in shops, movie houses, hotels, theatres and restaurants: DON'T WORRY ABOUT THE CASH! WE'LL TAKE YOUR CHECK! Department stores urged customers to use their charge accounts, and if they had none, to open one. On the whole, an air of desperate good humor prevailed in the United States.

"I was reminded of the grim jokes we used to make on the way up to the front during the war," wrote a newspaper columnist who had been a combat soldier.

The New Deal's first shot hit the target dead center. The bank closings established strong confidence in Roosevelt. FDR had shown the people he was not afraid to act.

At the same time that he issued the bank proclamation, the President also called a special session of Congress for Thursday, March 9. When Congress convened, FDR demanded and received legislation to regulate banking, currency and foreign exchange. But this was only the beginning. In about one hundred days, the special session of Congress passed Roosevelt-sponsored legislation at a record clip. Only in wartime had any President so dominated Congress and even then, never so completely. Everything Roosevelt wanted, Congress hastened to grant.

During those frenetic hundred days, Congress enacted the National Industrial Recovery Act (NRA) for industrial reform; the Agricultural Adjustment Act (AAA) to control crop surpluses and farm prices; the Securities Act regulating banking and finance; the Unemployment Relief Act, which created the Civilian Conservation Corps (CCC) and gave to thousands of unemployed youths jobs planting trees, building dams and bridges, preventing and fighting forest fires and other useful conservation work.

Other legislation provided funds for federal relief payments to the unemployed. There was a Public Works Administration (PWA) with an appropriation of $3,300,000 to be spent on new highways, bridges, public buildings and similar projects. At a later date the function of the PWA was taken over by the Works Projects Administration (WPA) which provided employment for writers, actors, directors, artists, dancers, musicians, teachers and other creative people as well as skilled and non-skilled laborers.

Roosevelt also secured from Congress a bill creating the Tennessee Valley Authority (TVA) whose ambitious purpose was to develop government-owned power plants throughout the Tennessee Valley, bringing electricity to one of the most backward areas in the nation.

The list of legislative enactments during the first hundred days of the Roosevelt Era was a stupendous one. The laws covered every phase of the nation's social and economic life— even to the legalization of beer as a prelude for prohibition repeal. A historian noted that the laws passed by the special session of Congress would ordinarily have been produced by "an entire generation of legislators . . ."

The President did not spare himself once he was established in office. From March through June 1933, FDR made ten major speeches including several radio broadcasts to the nation. These intimate talks, which became known as "fireside chats," wove a bond between the Man In The White House and the Man In The Street. FDR's customary salutation was, "My friends and fellow Americans," after which he launched into a lucid explanation of his activities.

In addition to all the speeches, Roosevelt sent fifteen messages to Congress and supervised the enactment of at least fifteen important laws—all during the same hundred-day period. The people had longed for a man of action. They now had one—with a vengeance. FDR was an incredibly hard worker, literally bristling with energy. An aide once remarked of him: "All that energy; all that vitality! Why, he's a human dynamo!"

During those early months of the New Deal, not only the President but his "Brain Trust" and cabinet as well went full speed long hours every day. Any man who could not stand the grueling pace was dropped. It was a vivid and exciting time; the very air of Washington crackled as the New Deal mobilized for its assault on the Depression.

The staid capital was unused to so much bustle and fervor. These New Dealers were different from the stodgy politicians who had for so many years held sway in Washington. The New Dealers were young, vibrant and intense. They bubbled with ideas, suggestions, theories and philosophies. These bright-eyed, enthusiastic Democrats came to the capital in droves, each seeking a place in the administration. The job hunters hounded Postmaster General James Farley, the administration's chief patronage dispenser "like wolves on the prowl," according to a newspaper reporter.

Experts, specialists, lawyers, judges, engineers, bankers, businessmen and labor union leaders rushed to Washington in those fervent days. Everyone wanted an audience with FDR. Everyone had a suggestion or a plan for ending the Depression.

The lights burned late every night in the rapidly expanding government offices that spring of 1933. Men waded through mounds of paper work, wrote and rewrote bills, laws and opinions. It was as though the nation was being created afresh and the capital was enjoying a rebirth. Office structures were rising all over Washington. The new government agencies needed room. The clattering of carpenters' hammers could be heard around the clock. Bricklayers, structural steelworkers, masons, plumbers and electricians who only months before had been hopelessly unemployed were now working overtime. The rapping of hammers, the whine of bandsaws, the staccato bursts of riveters, the clash of cement mixers—all the noises and clamor of construction were welcome sounds in a city which for so long had been shrouded in the tomblike silence of defeat.

America itself was reacting to the stimulus of the New Deal. The nation was stirring with hope. Even the wretched dwellers of squalid Hoovervilles all over the land crawled out of the darkness. Perhaps, soon, they would not be among the forgotten men. Perhaps their ordeal was ending and the Depression would one day be only a hideous memory.

⌐ 8

"Who's Afraid of the Big Bad Wolf?"

The United States reacted to the New Deal's ministra-
tions like a sick person responding to a miracle drug. The
nation took the New Deal medicine, stirred, sat up and
looked about with undimmed eyes. That spring and summer
the young men were gathering in the CCC camps. As federal
work projects got under way, inroads were made into cutting
down the ranks of the unemployed. Jobs began opening in
private industry as well.

Further signs of recovery were apparent in the stock market
where speculators drifted back to try their luck as an upturn
in prices heralded another bullish trend.

Having won the first skirmishes, the administration turned
to other pressing affairs. The President appointed General
Hugh Johnson, an ex-cavalry officer, as head of the National
Recovery Act (NRA) to establish prices, labor codes and fair
practices for each industry.

Some businessmen and manufacturers were reluctant to cooperate with the government, and Johnson dealt personally with them. "They stood before him in uneasy groups like so many captured soldiers," wrote a reporter, "and listened meekly as the general slapped them into line."

Johnson used varied tactics. He bullied, cajoled, argued, threatened and reasoned. And he got results. The NRA became the greatest mass effort in the United States since the Liberty Bond Drives of World War days.

The big Blue Eagle, symbol of the NRA, was displayed everywhere—on stickers, banners, flags and billboards. Everywhere one saw the NRA slogan: "We Do Our Part!"

Industrial re-employment posed problems. Since the onset of the Depression, factory methods had greatly improved. Labor-saving devices had replaced men. In farming areas there was still unrest and occasional disorder. The New Deal's higher farm price levels and the benefits of the Agricultural Adjustment Act (AAA) had not yet become effective. There were still some current troubles, but the future seemed brighter. Disgruntled workers and discontented farmers held their tempers because it wasn't fair to get mad at a government trying to help.

The mood of the nation was changing. Every setback was no longer regarded as a calamity. The jittery, demoralized people were calming down under Roosevelt's firm leadership. His smiling confidence reassured them. There was nothing to fear but fear itself. And after a few brief months of the New Deal, Americans were less afraid. The Depression could be licked—of that they were convinced.

No wonder everyone went around whistling a catchy tune from Walt Disney's newest picture, *The Three Little Pigs:* "Who's Afraid of the Big Bad Wolf?" This was quite a step

151

forward for people whose theme song only a short time ago had been "Brother, Can You Spare A Dime?"

It would take a long time to restore the nation's prosperity, but FDR had already accomplished one of the most important things—he had revived American morale. People were beginning to be optimistic, to think in terms of progress, not retrogression.

The repeal of prohibition on December 5, 1933, was a milestone in the right direction. It symbolized a complete break with the heritage of the Roaring Twenties, that deceptively disastrous Harding-Coolidge era during which the seeds of the Depression had been sown. It seemed incredible in 1933 that any large segment of the American public ever could have been seriously concerned over prohibition.

Americans were emerging from the terrible Depression, but they learned one simple and obvious truth which had been forgotten during the lush years of the 1920's—no man was insulated enough or secure enough to escape the mass fate. What happened to one in a democracy eventually happened to all. If democracy was to work, the good things of life could not be monopolized only by the strong, the swift, the ruthless. The American people learned from the Depression that anyone could become a "forgotten man" at any time.

And out of this crucible the nation achieved a greater social consciousness. The aged had to be looked after; the unemployed must not be ignored nor the country's young people wasted. From this rising social awareness emerged the New Deal's old-age pensions, unemployment insurance and other like benefits.

In the 1930's, what once had been scorned was now looked upon as a necessity. The most unyielding adherent of "rugged individualism" no longer argued against federal aid to the weak, the helpless, the unfortunate. In the shared national suffering of the Depression, the American people had rediscovered compassion.

9

"...the honeymoon days
are over...."

When FDR first took office, few men questioned his moves. Almost every American was grateful that a strong leader had taken charge of the foundering ship.

Once it became apparent that the country could survive the crisis, a current of opposition to Roosevelt began flowing. Even within his own party, Roosevelt had enemies. These conservative Democrats disapproved of many New Deal policies but had gone along with the tide. Republican congressmen and senators had supported Roosevelt's measures, fearing complete isolation from the voters if they followed any other course.

But as 1933 waned, with everyone more complacent now that the United States had been miraculously saved, the President's foes gathered the courage to speak out against him—timidly at first, then with growing boldness and venom.

Radicals claimed he was moving too slowly. Conservatives said that he was going too fast. Both left and right accused him of seeking to establish a dictatorship, but neither could agree on just what sort of dictatorship it was.

"Communist!" conservatives called FDR.

"Fascist!" Communists labeled him.

All through 1934 and 1935, the President was the target of such confused criticism. About the only truth in the flood of disapproval swirling around him was the fact that the New Deal was not functioning smoothly or with complete success.

For instance, the NRA, less than a year since its enactment, was floundering. This was because businessmen generally adopted a policy of sabotage toward the NRA. While they objected to the law in its entirety, the main source of their irritation was Section 7a, which gave workers the right to organize into unions for the purpose of collective bargaining. This seemed an open invitation by the government for all workers to unionize. However, the NRA gave the administration no power to force employers to either recognize or even deal with the unions.

As a result, violent strikes broke out in the summer of 1934 as workers tried to attain their rights under Section 7a. The city of San Francisco was paralyzed by a general stoppage in July 1934. A textile walkout which spread to seven southern states brought bloodshed when strikers fought scabs, police and National Guardsmen.

It was an unhappy time for the administration. Both sides involved in the labor struggles attacked the President. The workers complained that after encouraging them to organize, Roosevelt was not backing them in their crusade for union conditions. On the other hand, employers bitterly accused the President not only of practically fomenting the strikes, but also of throwing the government's weight with the unions.

President Roosevelt bore all the criticism with good humor and restraint. Once, when the double-edged condemnations were particularly harsh during that restive, strike-torn summer of 1934, he grinned at an aide: "It's unsafe for me to say anything these days, but I can tell you, without rousing a hornets' nest, that the honeymoon days are over. From now on, we'll have to fight like the devil for every piece of legislation we want."

FDR had correctly estimated the situation. His comparatively easy honeymoon period with both Congress and the public was over. But he enjoyed a good, knock-down political brawl. He worked hard for every enactment he proposed, and so astutely did he conduct himself that despite the hostile bloc in Congress, all the legislation he either originated or backed in 1934–1935 was passed.

More disturbing to the President than private and congressional opposition to his policies was the sluggish pace of recovery after the first few searing months. Somehow, nothing the administration did could stimulate a swift rush to the summit of prosperity. The national economy had made a startling comeback from the bank-panic doldrums of early 1933 when the New Deal was instituted. But soon after that first dash ahead, the economy stumbled and slipped downward.

Then, suddenly, swiftly, catastrophe struck the farmlands of the Middle West. On November 11, 1933, when Armistice Day ceremonies were being observed across the nation, a bitter gale swept out over the Great Plains in a region that stretched from the Texas Panhandle all the way to South Dakota.

November gales were not a rarity in that part of the country, but no living man had ever seen a storm such as the one in 1933. The wind came on like a moving black cloud darkened by the tons of dust it carried. The Black Blizzard, men called the storm.

According to one eyewitness the Black Blizzard was "even blacker than night, because one can see through night. . . . It was a wall of dirt one's eyes could not penetrate, but it could penetrate the eyes, ears, nose . . . and lungs until one coughed up black. . . . When the wind died and the sun shone forth again, it was on a different world. There were no fields . . . only black sand drifting into huge mounds out of which poked the roofs of sheds, the chimneys of houses, the weather vanes of barns. . . . It was a world buried under the wind-driven dirt drifts."

The Black Blizzard spread ruin and devastation through a tremendous farming belt. But that storm was only the first in a cycle of similar dust storms on the heels of a three-year-long drought. In some parts of South Dakota, Kansas and Oklahoma, there had been no rain for months. The dry spell turned top soil to powdery dust which was picked up by the winds and carried off in swirling, destructive clouds.

The storms transformed the farmlands of the afflicted regions into a veritable desert. There were dunes of black sands where wheat, barley and corn had once waved in the breezes. The dust choked livestock, filled wells, killed crops, buried cultivated fields. Roads, farm buildings, schools, homes and even telegraph poles vanished beneath the black mounds. What had once been known as the nation's "breadbasket" was now called the "Dust Bowl."

This upheaval of nature caused terrible hardships among farmers and created thousands of refugees who fled the stricken Dust Bowl. They moved westward to the fertile

157

lands of California, in battered cars, hoping to find work picking crops. It was this pitiful migration that John Steinbeck described in his novel *The Grapes of Wrath*. The plight of these "Okies," as the wanderers were scornfully called by farmers outside the Dust Bowl, was one of the most tragic in the unhappy story of the Depression.

The government helped the migrants as best it could; camps were established for them, but the federal centers could not house all the refugees. Most of them existed under abominable conditions, toiling as crop-pickers at slave wages.

And, a short time later, as though the drought and the Dust Bowl were mere preliminaries to what nature had in store, the country suffered a series of disastrous floods throughout New England and the Midwest. The great industrial center of Pittsburgh was inundated as flood waters raged through the city's heart. Cincinnati was engulfed by a mountainous "wall of water."

But, while the dust storms and the floods were the work of rampaging nature, in a sense, these were man-made disasters as well. For too many years, the American people had squandered the nation's natural resources—the forests, the grasslands, the streams. Arable soil was cultivated until it would no longer bear crops. The fallow land was then abandoned, and what had once been fine topsoil was now lumpy dirt. No one worried about irrigation or crop rotation. It was a big country with lots of land. For generations the non-producing fields had gone to seed. The land had been misused and abused. Cattle grazed on the grassy plains until wide regions were denuded. The forests and water sheds which could have prevented the floods were stripped by the woodsman's ax or burned out by preventable forest fires. In all the years, only ardent conservationists paid any attention to the despoiling of the land.

"Why worry about a few trees? There's plenty more out yonder," the Americans said. But one day, there no longer was an "out yonder." And when the rains had swollen the rivers and the waters raged out of control there were no trees, grass, or woodlands to sponge up the flood waters. Too late, the people wept; too late, they regretted the wasteful decades.

Roosevelt saw flood control and soil and forest conservation as a part of the war against the Depression. Disregarding his critics, he ramrodded through Congress a series of appropriations for PWA flood control projects. At the same time, the CCC boys were put to work planting seedlings and protecting the forests. For the first time, the federal government was actively concerned about conserving the natural resources of the country.

During the latter part of his first term, Roosevelt often came to grips with his political enemies. Some were strong. One of the foremost was Senator Huey Long, whose "Share Our Wealth" program was drawing followers like "spilled molasses draws blue-bottle flies" as the Louisiana demagogue described the growth of his movement. A poll conducted in late 1935 by the Democratic National Committee revealed the disturbing fact that Long commanded more than 4,000,000 votes if he should decide to make a bid for the Presidency.

The Louisiana senator appealed to the mob mentality. Ruthless, iron-fisted and power hungry, Long gave a promise of menace in Depression-shaken America. His cry "Every Man a King!" aroused the downtrodden. His disregard for civil rights and individual liberties marked him as a potential dictator, a destroyer of democracy. Long cared nothing for democracy—he knew that his utopian plan of $5,000 a year for all meant more to his followers than all the benefits of democracy.

Not so dangerous as Long, but still posing a political threat to Roosevelt and the New Deal was the Townsend Plan, which rallied to its standards several million aged persons— an unofficial estimate of its membership was in the neighborhood of 10,000,000. Political observers believed Dr. Townsend controlled at least 3,000,000 votes.

The New Deal was assailed by labor, big business, Huey Long's rabble and Townsend's oldsters; but these were not its only enemies. Far to the left were the Communists—the gravest threat to the New Deal. Though small in numbers, the American Communist party was militant and boasted a shrewd, aggressive leadership. The party's influence extended far beyond its 75,000 membership. Communists were adept at taking over other groups and using prominent persons as dupes to further disguise Communist causes. Some of labor's most skillful leaders were also members of the Communist party. Communist union organizers won recruits for the party by their daring and boldness in organizing workers whom conservative AFL chiefs had ignored in the past.

The Communists fomented strikes, led demonstrations of unemployed, made noisy demands for increased social security and unemployment insurance and agitated against capitalism, with the New Deal as a special target. They maligned Roosevelt because he sought to shore up "the vicious and doomed system of capitalism" instead of wholeheartedly siding with the working class in what the Communists called "the coming irreconcilable conflict of the class struggle between capital and labor."

160

During 1934 and 1935, the Communists smeared as a Fascist any liberal who did not come out for "class war" and the overthrow of the capitalist system. While the Communist doctrine of class war and the "dictatorship of the proletariat" was alien to the American viewpoint, it still attracted many people—not only embittered Depression victims but intellectuals, students, journalists, writers, actors and professionals, as well.

Despite these assaults from left, right and center, the New Deal remained intact. Once, in a jocular mood, Roosevelt likened himself to a quarterback running a football team. "I call for this play—if it fails, I call for that, and if they stop me on the ground—why, I call for a forward pass," he laughed.

The President handled his foes adroitly. He placated labor leaders, soothed businessmen, mollified this group, pacified that one. Against the loud and vociferous Communists, FDR did nothing; he welcomed their criticism. "The more the Communists howl, the more positive I am that I have found the road to a secure future for our country," Roosevelt told an interviewer.

However, in the summer of 1935, Communist attacks on Roosevelt ceased entirely. Moscow, fearing the rising power of Hitler and Mussolini, called for Communists of every land to unite with liberals in a popular front against Nazism and Fascism. With this new line of attack, the Communists in the United States suddenly saw FDR not as a "social Fascist" but as a "fighting progressive."

Huey Long still proved troublesome, but he was eliminated in September 1935, when a disgruntled former follower assassinated "The Kingfish," as he was called. Without his

161

dynamic leadership, the "Share Our Wealth" movement fell apart and another New Deal enemy was silenced.

Of all the antagonists of the New Deal, the United States Supreme Court was the most powerful. On May 27, 1935, the Court ruled the NRA to be unconstitutional on the grounds that Congress had transferred legislative power to the executive. Under the Constitution, the Court declared, the federal government might regulate only interstate commerce. In the unanimous view of the justices, the NRA dealt with matters such as wages, hours and working conditions which could not properly be considered interstate commerce.

According to the decision, the federal government had no right to regulate working conditions, hours and wages as it had done in the NRA. This ruling was a body blow to the New Deal; the NRA was one of its mainstays. President Roosevelt, irked by the Court's action, called the NRA decision a "relic of horse and buggy jurisprudence."

However, FDR did not at that time take any action against the Court. At his behest, Congress passed the National Labor Relations Act, better known as the Wagner Act for Senator Robert Wagner who sponsored the bill. The Wagner Act, which became effective in July 1935, guaranteed workers the right to collective bargaining through unions of their own choice. Employers were specifically forbidden to discriminate against union members or to support company-formed unions.

The law was to be enforced and supervised by a three-member National Labor Relations Board (NLRB) which, if necessary, would hold elections for workers to pick the union they wanted. The board also heard complaints of workers whose rights had been violated.

Reactionary employers fought hard against the Wagner

Act and confidently looked to the Supreme Court to declare it unconstitutional. But in a sudden and startling reversal, the Court upheld the Wagner Act on the basis that workers had a "fundamental right" to organize and that unions were "essential to give workers opportunity to deal on an equality with their employer."

Although the Court had supported the administration in the Wagner Act, a time was approaching when the President and the high tribunal were destined to have a showdown. It was clear that FDR did not intend to let the Supreme Court undermine his New Deal by invalidating the laws he felt were needed to save the nation and bring the Depression to a finish.

☞ 10

"As Maine goes, so goes Vermont."

Suddenly and incredibly it was 1936. The four years of Roosevelt's term had sped past in a tumultuous blur. The United States, in 1936, was quite different from what it had been in 1932 when fear had chilled its heart.

Those awful days were now behind the American people. Bank failures, so frequent in 1932, seldom occurred four years later. Gone, too, was the prospect of immediate economic collapse. The crises in banking, in currency stabilization and international finance had been successfully ended. Just as important, the American people no longer were demoralized. The fight against the Depression went slowly, but it went on. Unemployment was on the wane. The WPA and other New Deal creations provided useful work for millions. Bread lines were growing smaller. The Hoovervilles were nearly deserted.

The New Deal fought all the ills that had been infecting

the economy for half a century; it was a Herculean task the Roosevelt administration had undertaken. To accomplish it, the government poured millions of dollars into the economy through relief payments, federal works, bonuses to the war veterans (the battered Bonus Expeditionary Force had finally won its fight) and other sources.

Although the Republicans harped on "government extravagance," not even they could honestly deny the necessity that drove the administration to do what had been done. Even Republican arch-conservatives might not have acted differently. The federal government had to spend money if the nation was to survive. The major difference between the Republicans and the Democrats was the full speed with which the latter moved, while the former wanted slower action.

Life in the United States had drastically been altered since 1932. The five-day work week was now universal. Unemployment insurance and old-age pensions were no longer regarded as "socialistic" trends. There was a general liberalization in thought, dress and behavior. The people of 1936 had become conditioned to new ideas, new ways and new concepts.

Outside the United States, the world had also changed. After only three years of existence, the Nazi government of Germany was rapidly becoming the dominant force in Europe. Hitler had scrapped the Versailles Treaty, marched back into the Rhineland and the Saar and prepared for a series of territorial claims which would keep the Continent in a turmoil of war fever another three years.

Germany blatantly began to rearm. "Guns not butter!" Hitler cried to the German people.

"Sieg Heil!" the Germans roared in approval.

165

The arms race was on. When Germany forged more weapons, an international rearmament got under way. This revived the national economies of various countries as the manufacture of war materiel resulted in ever-growing employment. In England, France, Belgium, Holland—in most of Europe—many wondered whether this half-war was not preferable to a peacetime during which millions of working people were starving.

Hitler went on with his aggressive intentions, defying the League of Nations to stop him. But that moribund body had already shown its weakness by failing to halt the Japanese attacks on Manchuria and China. Emboldened by the feckless action of the League in dealing with Japan, Benito Mussolini, the Fascist dictator of Italy, launched an invasion of Ethiopia while the League of Nations stood helplessly by wringing its hands over the moral injustices of *Il Duce*'s act.

The whole world could see that the League of Nations, after only sixteen years of life, was now in its death throes. The failures of 1920 had come full circle by 1936. Only eighteen years from the end of World War I, humbled Germany was readying its revenge. The haughty victors, England and France, looked on in awe as Hitler created the most powerful war machine the world had ever known.

In the summer of 1936, a civil war erupted against the Spanish Republic. A clique of Fascist generals headed by Francisco Franco led the uprising. Hitler and Mussolini supplied Franco with tanks, arms, planes and troops. Soviet Russia sided with the Republic, and Spain became a battleground of the struggle between Fascism and Communism. But Italian and German help was far greater than Russian aid and Franco's legions closed in on Madrid.

Meanwhile, the democracies stood aside and allowed

166

Hitler and Mussolini to have their way in Spain. England and France proposed a non-intervention policy to which both Germany and Italy subscribed but at the same time continued to supply Franco with arms. Both *Il Duce* and *Der Fuehrer* knew they could get away with almost anything—the democracies feared another war; 1914–1918 had scarred the victors even worse than the losers. While England and France shunned any action, the Nazis and the Fascists felt free to do as they pleased. Thus the march of aggression went on unimpeded in Europe as the Continent gradually darkened under the gathering war clouds.

Not even the weak-spined governments of England and France could allow Germany and Italy to run roughshod over all Europe. Somewhere a stand would have to be taken—but that day was still distant, and obviously, the deadline did not lie in Spain.

Amid such crackling tensions, the American presidential election of 1936 approached. The Democrats ran FDR and John Nance Garner for a second term. The Republicans picked a dark horse, Alfred Mossman Landon, the governor of Kansas. His running mate was Frank Knox. Landon, who was promptly labeled the "Kansas Coolidge," ran on a platform dedicated to saving the country by what he called "The American Way" but which was studded with many New Deal reforms. For instance, the Republicans still kept unemployment insurance, old-age benefits, public works and certain aspect of Roosevelt's farm program.

Landon had influential support, particularly from a group of multimillionaires who had banded together in an organization known as the Liberty League. Many discontented Democrats, opposed to the New Deal, also backed Landon.

The "Kansas Coolidge" was a game, but colorless campaigner. His speeches, delivered in flat, nasal, midwestern tones, did not compare with Roosevelt's flamboyant style. He could stir no real public enthusiasm despite the efforts of the press which was dominantly pro-Republican. One newspaper chain ran a daily bannerline: "A Vote For Roosevelt Is a Vote for Communism!"

FDR campaigned with customary gusto. He pointed out the advances that had been made during the four years of his administration. Admittedly, unemployment was high—some 9,000,000 were still jobless—but this was an appreciable drop from the 14,000,000 who had been workless in 1932. More jobs were opening daily. Factories were getting back into operation. Farmers no longer faced wholesale bankruptcy.

The flood control and soil conservation programs of the New Deal were in full swing. Soon the Dust Bowl would be a receding nightmare and the rampaging rivers a forgotten danger. Roosevelt also reminded the voters that banks were now secure, stock market manipulations were at a minimum, and investors had federal laws to protect them from stock frauds.

"We have made progress!" Roosevelt declared. "And progress, even with mistakes, beats standing still and marking time!"

As Election Day came closer, FDR's enemies launched a whispering campaign designed to turn the voters against him. The rumormongers spread malicious lies: The President was losing his mind; he had fainting spells and temper tantrums; his health was shattered; he had been stricken by successive heart attacks; he was meeting with Communists; he had suffered a stroke. On and on ran the cruel whispers.

The Liberty Leaguers spared no money in their efforts to

168

get FDR out of the White House. A daily stream of anti-Roosevelt propaganda spewed out of radio loudspeakers and filled the newspapers.

But on Election Day it was the people who had the final say. They ran up 27,761,507 votes for Roosevelt while Landon gathered only 16,679,583. Two states, Maine and Vermont, went to the Republicans as Roosevelt took forty-six states to gain 523 electoral votes against Landon's 8.

This lopsided victory elicited a wry comment from Roosevelt's campaign manager, Jim Farley. It had been a political truism for years in the United States that "As Maine goes, so goes the nation." Farley paraphrased this to: "As Maine goes, so goes Vermont."

The election result was an overwhelming mandate for the President and the New Deal. As always, under democracy, the vital decisions were made by the people in the voting booths.

169

11

"The law is on our side..."

There was a cloudburst in Washington, D.C., on January 20, 1937—a deluge of rain which inundated the entire eastern half of the United States. It had been raining this way for more than a week. In spite of the foul weather, a huge crowd had assembled in Capitol Square for Franklin Delano Roosevelt's second inauguration.

Unlike the first time he had been sworn into office, the dripping skies did not turn clear, the sun did not burst forth. The crowd shifted uncomfortably as gusty winds tore at umbrellas and drove the cold, slanting rain. It was a day to have stayed home along with the millions waiting at radios to hear the President's inaugural address. But ardent New Deal adherents were not daunted by rain or discomfort. They stood in the downpour and cheered Roosevelt when he appeared at noon on a platform festooned with dripping bunting and sodden banners. Marine Corps bandsmen, rainwater dripping from their instruments, greeted his arrival with a watery rendition of "Hail to the Chief."

Bareheaded despite the rain, Roosevelt stood squarely before Chief Justice Charles Evans Hughes and repeated the oath that made him President of the United States for another four years. The wet, shivering audience watched in fascination as FDR and the Chief Justice confronted each other. Everyone in that vast throng wondered whether the President was going to touch on the Supreme Court in his inaugural speech.

Twenty months had passed since the invalidation of the NRA and Roosevelt had remained silent. Now, re-elected with a resounding majority, would he still maintain that silence, or would he speak his mind about the Court's role in blocking the New Deal program?

That question was quickly answered. He made no mention of the Supreme Court in his eloquent and moving inaugural address. Instead he spoke of the paradox which brought misery and poverty to so many millions living in the world's richest nation. He spoke of the need to keep on fighting against this blight. Harking back to 1933, Roosevelt traced the victories won in four years.

"Shall we pause now and turn our back on the road that lies ahead?" he asked.

As the last echoes of his resonant voice died away, a thunderous ovation rose from the crowds below in Capitol Square. The cheers drowned out the wind and the rain. The people felt a bond between themselves and the President. His hopes were theirs. His dreams were theirs.

The future gleamed brightly, but the road was a toilsome one. Even after four years of constant struggle, the Depression still poisoned the nation. Its marks lingered in every part of the country. Pinch-faced children still shuffled to school in patched clothing and torn shoes. Men still huddled

171

on park benches. Hunger and misery still touched many lives.

But in that rainstorm, the President had again sounded the call to a battle that would not end until the last vestiges of the Depression had been erased from every corner of the land.

To some, the rainfall on Inauguration Day must have seemed an ill omen. In a way it was, for that storm, which had followed others and would be followed by even more severe downpours, fed the waters of the Ohio River and set the stage for a terrible flood.

Even as Roosevelt spoke, halfway across the country, in Flint, Michigan, thousands of auto workers were conducting a strike against the General Motors Corporation (GMC), the giant of the automobile industry. The strikers were using a tactic strange to the American labor movement. In the past, striking workers had left the factories and set up picket lines around the plants.

The General Motors strikers did not follow that procedure. Instead of leaving the struck shops, the workers simply sat down at their machines and took possession of the plant. Sympathizers on the outside supplied them with food, and the stay-ins defied every attempt to dislodge them from GMC property.

The corporation, which employed more than 250,000 men and manufactured some 2,000,000 cars and trucks annually, had been virtually paralyzed since December 1936, by sit-down strikes in their Flint, Michigan, plants.

The stoppage at General Motors was the first major battle in a widespread industrial war which was soon to affect many thousands of American workers as the labor unions launched the greatest organizational drive ever known in the United States.

The GMC strike was led by the United Automobile Workers Union (UAW), which was affiliated with the Committee for Industrial Organization (CIO), a new and aggressive labor federation that had been set up to rival the American Federation of Labor (AFL). In 1935, certain AFL leaders, dissatisfied with the slow-moving machinery of the old federation, had created the CIO to spur organization of unions in all industries. The chief driving force in forming the CIO was bushy-browed John L. Lewis, head of the United Mine Workers Union (UMW).

When the NRA was passed in 1933, giving the workers the right to collective bargaining, it was Lewis who had thundered at an AFL convention that the time had come to "organize the unorganized." The stodgy AFL chieftains hesitated and temporized. They made excuses but took no action. No major unionization effort was launched.

Short-tempered John L. Lewis lost his patience. Risking every penny in the United Mine Workers' treasury, he began a gigantic campaign to enroll new members. At a meeting of his organizers, Lewis pointed to Section 7a of the NRA and cried, "There's nothing in God's world to stop you now! Go out in the field, sign up the men! For once, labor has clear sailing! The law is on our side!"

After the Supreme Court invalidated the NRA and the National Labor Relations Act took its place in 1935, Lewis increased his efforts. The UMW's organizing drive had had signal success, and other labor leaders, such as Sidney Hillman of the Amalgamated Clothing Workers, David Dubinsky of the International Ladies' Garment Workers, and Charles P. Howard of the International Typographers Union, met with Lewis on October 9, 1935, to form the Committee for Industrial Organization, within the framework of the AFL. However, CIO and AFL could not live under the same roof. The latter clung to traditional, old-fashioned craft unionism: each trade banded together into separate unions so that an industry such as the automobile, which employed many categories of workers—electricians, carpenters, machinists, upholsterers and a host of others—might have a dozen or more craft unions within one shop. On the other hand, the CIO proposed to organize all workers in the same industry within one big union, regardless of craft or specialty.

This basic difference in philosophy soon caused a rift between adherents of craft and industrial unionism. As the rift grew wider, the executive committee of the AFL finally expelled all unions affiliated with the CIO. In the fall of 1936, with John L. Lewis as its head, the CIO became a militant, hard-hitting labor federation ready to fight for decent working conditions in any industry.

The General Motors workers proved fertile ground for CIO agitation. The men had many just complaints: wages were low, work was seasonal, and the speed-up on the production lines was unbearable. United Auto Worker organizers met with overwhelming response among the GMC men, and before long, the UAW had enough strength to tackle the mammoth corporation. William S. Knudsen of General Motors refused to treat with the union and in December 1936, the sit-down strikes began.

The company resorted to force after peaceful efforts had failed to dislodge the strikers. But neither tear gas, police clubs nor buckshot could rout the embattled workers. They held the plants with the determination of besieged soldiers defending a crucial strongpoint. Time after time, attacking

174

police were driven off under a barrage of wheel bolts, pipe handles and tire tools.

This labor warfare raged until February 3, when Knudsen finally gave in and agreed to meet with representatives of the union. A week later, the UAW triumphantly announced that GMC recognized the union as the exclusive bargaining agent for its workers and would negotiate a contract with the UAW.

The CIO had won a tremendous and significant victory. As a result of the GMC strike, sit-down strikers all over the country took over factories, five-and-ten-cent stores, department stores, laundries, machine shops—every sort of business —until by May 1937, more than 500,000 workers had participated in sit-downs.

The next important CIO target was the sprawling U.S. Steel Corporation, monolith of the industry. A special unit, the Steel Workers Organizing Committee (SWOC) under an inspired leader, Phil Murray, was created to take on U.S. Steel.

Strangely enough, the corporation surrendered without a fight. This capitulation astounded both capital and labor, for U.S. Steel had long been an implacable foe of unions. The decision to sign with the SWOC had not resulted in any change of attitude by U.S. Steel management; it was done for practical considerations only. The company had a huge backlog of foreign orders for armament steel and did not wish to risk endangering delivery because of a strike.

Labor was exultant at this second successive CIO masterstroke. John L. Lewis boasted that all the steel companies would fall into line now that the SWOC had "Big Steel" in its pocket.

But Lewis spoke too soon. A number of the smaller steel

corporations, known as "Little Steel"—National, Inland, Bethlehem and Youngstown Sheet and Tube—formed a pact not to negotiate with the CIO. A strike resulted and "Little Steel" fought the union.

The strikers were treated with undue brutality. The companies spent millions to break the walkout. They hired gunmen to intimidate the workers. Professional strikebreakers were flown in to smash the picket lines. There were bloody clashes almost daily outside Little Steel company plants.

The worst and most unnecessary violence took place on Memorial Day, 1937, in South Chicago near the Republic Steel Mill. A crowd of strikers, assembled in an open field for a mass meeting, was suddenly attacked by company guards and Chicago police. Tear gas, fire hoses and nightsticks scattered the strikers. Then, without provocation, police officers and guards opened fire on the fleeing people. Before the shooting ended, ten persons were dead of bullet wounds in the back, and ninety more had been wounded by gunfire.

A wave of indignation and protest broke on Little Steel. "Fascists! Murderers!" screamed the Communists trying to stir public wrath. "See what workers can expect from capitalist exploiters? A bullet in the back!"

Not only the Communists, but every shade of political, religious and social opinion showed its disapproval of the Memorial Day tragedy. But Tom M. Girdler, head of Republic Steel and spokesman for Little Steel, stubbornly declared: "I won't have a contract verbal or written with the CIO. . . . I am not going to do it!"

Girdler's intransigence and Little Steel's terror tactics finally prevailed. The strike was broken and the CIO dropped

back in temporary defeat. But the lost encounter was merely a battle—the war was not yet over.

At the same time, as the growing CIO and the unyielding employers locked in bitter struggles, President Roosevelt, only two weeks after his second inauguration, made his play against the Supreme Court. He dropped a bombshell by proposing a reorganization of the high tribunal. He suggested that the Court be augmented and enlarged to fifteen judges rather than the current nine.

It was Roosevelt's opinion that the "Nine Old Men" who sat on the bench and gave the final word on the nation's legal affairs were attempting to throttle the New Deal. To prevent this, he recommended that whenever a Supreme Court justice passed the age of seventy without retiring and after having served at least ten years, the President should have the power to appoint an additional judge to assist him.

FDR took this step because he sincerely believed that the nine august judges, appointed as they were for life, had grown out of touch with the harsh realities of the 1930's. Their interpretations of the Constitution were too conservative and harked back to an earlier, more stable time in American history.

The President was suggesting nothing unusual in asking Congress for a law to change the size of the Court—it had been done six times previously by past Presidents. However, FDR's plan aroused much acrimonious debate. He was accused of trying to become a dictator by "loading" the Supreme Court with "flunkies of his own choosing" according to an anti-Roosevelt senator. Criticism of FDR crossed party lines; both Republicans and Democrats lambasted him for "tampering with the Supreme Court."

That issue proved to be one of the President's few political

177

blunders. When it came to a vote in the Senate, his plan was roundly beaten. But the fight he had launched was not wholly without positive results. Even before the matter had come to a vote in the Senate, the Supreme Court amazed both Roosevelt and the nation by a series of liberal decisions upholding much controversial New Deal legislation.

Then, as an aftermath to the President's setback in the Senate, seventy-odd-year-old Justice Willis Van Devanter, who had been on the bench since 1911, tendered his resignation in June 1937. This gave FDR the opportunity he needed to make an appointment to the Supreme Court. His choice was Senator Hugo L. Black of Alabama.

At the outset, this seemed an unfortunate selection. Justice Black admittedly had once briefly belonged to the Ku Klux Klan (KKK) in his home state. The revelation that a member of the Supreme Court had joined an organization dedicated to racial and religious intolerance stirred up a whirlwind. However, Justice Black lived down his past association by showing concern for civil liberties in his decisions and soon the furor about him died down.

Through the next few years FDR seated more liberal-minded judges on the Supreme Court as old-timers either died or resigned.

Thus, since 1933, the President had striven to end the Depression through fearless and liberal action. Much of the time he had to cope with fanatical resistance from those he called the "entrenched interests"—the giant corporations, the multimillionaire Liberty Leaguers, the reactionary politicians and the conservative bankers and financiers.

Not even Roosevelt's bitterest enemies doubted any longer that the New Deal had become a permanent part of the American life; it was here to stay. Slowly, the New Deal pulled the

nation out of the swamp of the Depression. So slowly at times that the progress was indiscernible, yet each painful gain was another step upward, another stride forward.

The Depression clung and made its presence known from time to time like a nagging toothache. And the Roosevelt administration added one agency after another to snuff out the signs of the Depression wherever they cropped up. An avalanche of alphabetized groups all but engulfed the American people: HOLC (Home Owners Loan Corporation), FHA (Federal Housing Administration), SEC (Securities and Exchange Commission), NYA (National Youth Administration), and dozens more, each with a specific function and a specific purpose, each adding to the anti-Depression fight.

Finally there were so many agencies that a presidential aide laughingly said, "I don't know whether I am dealing with government offices or alphabet soup."

But as the 1930's waned the attention of the United States was drawn to Europe. There, the failures of 1919 had come full circle. Germany was again rampant, with Hitler sending his rearmed legions on the march into Austria, the Sudetenland, Czechoslovakia and eastward to Danzig and the borders of Poland which he claimed as German soil.

The Civil War in Spain was running its tragic and bloody course; and the ugly thunderheads of a general conflict rumbled louder each day.

At last, after six years of sharpening crises, Hitler gave the order that started the Second World War. On September 1, 1939, German troops poured across the Polish frontiers. Two days later, England and France were at war with Germany.

The second great world conflict of the twentieth century had begun. Before it ended, millions upon millions of lives would be sacrificed; countless billions of dollars would be squandered in prosecuting the war; and, there would be few countries that had not engaged in the hostilities which ranged from the Arctic Circle to the farthest Pacific Islands.

The outbreak of World War II marked the end of an era for the United States. The dread Depression faded and disappeared by the close of 1939 as American industries and business began girding for the dark future. Defense and armament orders revitalized production and soon the forlorn shuffling of unemployed men was heard no more in the United States. The hunger, the broken spirits, the total demoralization of unemployment were no longer part of American life.

In 1940, when the Nazis overran the Low Countries and France, and England fought on alone, it was clear to most Americans that if democracy were to survive, Nazism and Fascism must be destroyed. The United States assumed the role of supplying the democracies with the tools of war. The Arsenal of Democracy, Winston Churchill called America.

That crucial year, 1940, the American people held a presidential election. FDR shattered precedent by seeking a third term, and the voters also broke with tradition by electing him. He won his victory over a worthy opponent, Wendell Willkie. It was a hard fight. Americans were sharply divided over the part the United States should play in the war. Many, including the hero of the 1920's Charles Lindbergh, belonged to an organization called "America First," which demanded this nation's complete isolation from the world's woes.

However, all arguments became academic on December 7, 1941, when Hitler's eastern ally, Japan, attacked the United States naval base at Pearl Harbor, Hawaii, with a surprise air raid, and America was plunged into the war which became truly global. No corner of the world was spared in this second World War.

That same generation which had endured the Depression now faced another shattering ordeal. The former CCC boys shouldered rifles instead of picks and shovels. The youth of America marched off to New Guinea and Italy, to France and Iwo Jima. They fought and some of them died.

But they had something worth fighting for and preserving: homes and jobs and freedom. Perhaps some of them wondered whether there would have been anything to fight for had America succumbed to the onslaught of the Great Depression and had a voice not rallied Americans with those burning words which still echoed through the long and difficult years: "The only thing we have to fear is fear itself."

Suggested Books
for Further Reading

In researching A NATION FIGHTS BACK, I consulted
many books, magazines, pamphlets, newspapers and other
sources. The books listed below do not comprise the total of
the works to which I referred; they are merely a sampling of
additional reading material that will, I feel, benefit anyone
who cares to further pursue the subject.

Allen, Frederick Lewis. *Only Yesterday*. New York: Harper
& Brothers, 1931.
——. *Since Yesterday*. New York: Harper & Brothers, 1939,
1940.
Grew, Joseph C. *Turbulent Era*. Boston: Houghton Mifflin
Co., 1952.
Hofstadter, Richard. *The Age of Reform*. New York: Alfred
A. Knopf, Inc., 1956.
Lynd, R. S. *Middletown in Transition*. New York: Harcourt,
Brace and Co., 1937.
Minton, Bruce, and Stuart, John. *The Fat Years and The
Lean*. New York: Modern Age Books, 1940.
Moley, Raymond. *After Seven Years*. New York: Harper &
Brothers, 1939.

Morris, Joe Alex. *What a Year!* New York: Harper & Brothers, 1956.

Parks, Henry B. *Recent America.* New York: Thomas Y. Crowell Co., 1945.

Rogers, Agnes. *I Remember Distinctly.* New York: Harper & Brothers, 1947.

Wector, Dixon. *The Age of the Great Depression.* New York: The Macmillan Co., 1948.

Weingast, David E. *Franklin D. Roosevelt: Man of Destiny.* New York: Julian Messner, Inc., 1952.

Index

184

191

About the Author

IRVING WERSTEIN is a native-born New
Yorker, still living in New York. He was
born on May 22, 1914, graduated from
Richmond Hill High School where he
was on the staff of the school paper. He
entered New York University in the
early '30's to study advertising copywrit-
ing, but family financial reverses necessi-
tated his leaving after two years. He has
been actor, waiter, camp counselor, factory worker, comedian, reporter. He sold
his first short story in 1938, and except
for a three-year stint in the Army, has
made writing a full-time career. He has
written radio and television scripts and
is the author of both adult and juvenile
books.

DUE